El Alamein 1942

The Turning of the Tide

Book 17

El Alamein 1942

The Turning of the Tide

First published in Great Britain in 2005 by Osprey Publishing, Midland House,
West Way, Botley, Oxford OX2 0PH, UK

This edition printed in 2009 by RBA Coleccionables, S.A., Pérez Galdós, 36.
08012 Barcelona, Spain by special arrangement with Osprey Publishing
and published as part of a series entitled Battles of World War II
by Hothouse Developments, Truman Building, 91 Brick Lane,
London E1 6QL, UK on behalf of RBA Coleccionables S.A.,
Pérez Galdós 36, 08012 Barcelona, Spain.

Produced under licence from Osprey Publishing Ltd.
ISSN 2040-0802

Printed in Spain by DÉDALO OFFSET
Distributed in the UK and ROI by COMAG,
Tavistock Road, West Drayton,Middlesex, UB7 7QE
www.comag.co.uk

CIP Data for this publication is available from the British Library.

Design: The Black Spot
Index by Alan Thatcher
Maps by The Map Studio
3D bird's eye views by The Black Spot

Imperial War Museum Collections
Many of the photos in this book come from the Imperial War Museum's huge
collections which cover all aspects of conflict involving Britain and the
Commonwealth since the start of the twentieth century. These rich resources
are available online to search, browse and buy at iwmcollections.org.uk
In addition to Collections Online, you can visit the Visitor Rooms where you can
explore over 8 million photographs, thousands of hours of moving images,
the largest sound archive of its kind in the world, thousands of diaries and
letters written by people in wartime, and a huge reference library.
To make an appointment, call (020) 7416 5320, or e-mail mail@iwm.org.uk
Imperial War Museum www.iwm.org.uk

Acknowledgements

I should like to express my gratitude to Pier Paolo Battistelli
and to LtCol Filippo Cappellano for the help they gave with
regard to photographs of the Italian forces of Panzerarmee
Afrika. Thanks also go to author Robin Neillands for
providing me with modern photographs of the battlefield.

Artist's note

Readers may care to note that the original paintings from
which the color plates in this book were prepared are
available for private sale. All reproduction copyright
whatsoever is retained by the publisher. All enquiries
should be addressed to:

Howard Gerrard
11 Oaks Road
Tenterden
Kent
TN30 6RD
UK

The Publishers regret that they can enter into no
correspondence upon this matter.

KEY TO MILITARY SYMBOLS

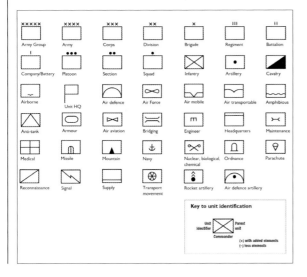

CONTENTS

ORIGINS OF THE BATTLE 7

CHRONOLOGY 12

OPPOSING COMMANDERS 15
British Commanders • Axis Commanders

OPPOSING ARMIES 20
British Forces • Axis Forces
Order of Battle: British Forces • Order of Battle: Axis Forces

OPPOSING PLANS 29

FIRST ALAMEIN 32

BATTLE OF ALAM HALFA 45

EL ALAMEIN: THE ATTACK 60

EL ALAMEIN: THE DOG FIGHT 71

EL ALAMEIN: BREAKOUT AND PURSUIT 83

THE BATTLEFIELD TODAY 92

BIBLIOGRAPHY 94

INDEX 95

INTRODUCTION

OPPOSITE: A Panzergrenadier
from Rommel's Afrika Korps, all
wrapped and goggled ready for
action against the enemy, wind-
blown sand and the unrelenting
sun. (Bundesarchiv 1011-785-
0285-14A)

The three battles which took place in the desert to the south of the isolated railway station of El Alamein in 1942 marked the climax of Hitler's plan to wrest Egypt from the British. His goal of seizing the Suez Canal and opening the Middle East to Axis forces had to be abandoned when his forces were soundly beaten. The success of these three actions transferred the initiative back to the British and precipitated the collapse of Generalfeldmarschall Erwin Rommel's Panzerarmee Afrika, forcing it into a long retreat across North Africa which eventually ended in its complete annihilation in Tunisia the following year. The final battle of El Alamein was a turning point in the war and was the last signal achievement gained by the British before American troops entered the conflict. Prime Minister Winston Churchill later claimed that before Alamein the British Army had not gained a major victory; after Alamein it did not suffer a major defeat.

The Desert War had begun as a colonial skirmish in September 1940 when Italian forces crossed the border from Libya into Egypt. The garrison of 36,000 British under Gen Wavell faced 215,000 Italians led by General Marshal Graziani. Undaunted by the overwhelming odds, Wavell's forces attacked the invaders and threw them out, following up the success with belligerent moves under LtGen O'Connor which pushed the Italians back across the whole of Cyrenaica to El Agheila. During the course of the final part of the advance, a British force of one armoured division and one infantry division completely destroyed an

The three architects of the
victory at El Alamein together
in Egypt in August 1942. From
left to right: Gen Sir Harold
Alexander (C-in-C Middle East),
Winston Churchill (British Prime
Minister) and LtGen Sir Bernard
Montgomery (Commander Eighth
Army). (IWM E15905)

enemy army of ten divisions, capturing 130,000 Italians, for the loss of 1,928 men killed, wounded and missing.

At this point, the British government decided to hold Cyrenaica with the smallest possible force while the rest of the army and air force concentrated in Egypt prior to a move to Greece to help stem the Axis troops who were trying to take over the country. Gen Wavell was against the move reasoning that a further advance through Libya could capture the port of Tripoli and evict Mussolini's Fascists from North Africa completely. He was overruled and valuable troops were sent to Greece, only to be unceremonially evicted by the Germans with considerable casualties.

Gen Erwin Rommel then arrived in North Africa on 12 February 1941 and, with a small force of German troops to stiffen Italian resolve, proceeded to push the depleted British force right back to the Egyptian border, leaving just the surrounded garrison in Tobruk as the only British left in Libya. This small German contribution to the Italian-sponsored campaign was gradually enlarged by new arrivals and eventually became the famed Afrika Korps comprising of 15th and 21st Panzer Divisions. It then became the backbone of the Italian–German army for the rest of the Desert War.

The British launched two attempts to push Rommel back and relieve Tobruk during the early part of 1941; both failed. Wavell was then replaced by Gen Claude Auchinleck as C-in-C Middle East. His forces in Egypt were designated British Eighth Army and placed under the command of Gen Alan Cunningham. In November 1941 Cunningham launched Operation *Crusader* against Rommel. It was not a great success. There followed a good deal of heavy fighting and much advance and retreat by both sides. Tobruk was relieved and Rommel at one point was pushed right back to El Agheila in Tripolitania where he first started. During the fighting, Auchinleck lost faith in the performance of Eighth Army's commander and replaced him with LtGen Neil Ritchie. At this point Auchinleck's position was weakened by the removal of British and Australian formations to the Far East to counter Japan's

EIGHTH ARMY RETREAT

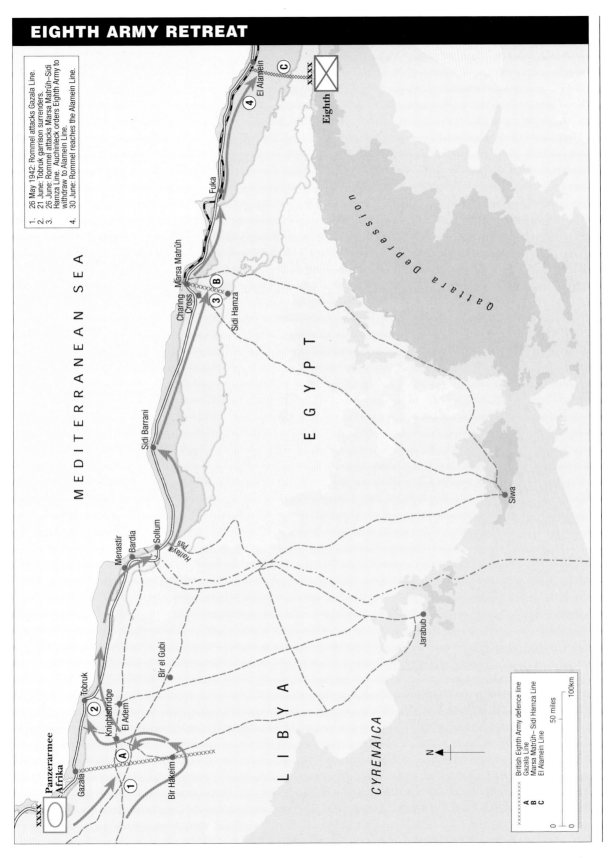

1. 26 May 1942: Rommel attacks Gazala Line.
2. 21 June: Tobruk garrison surrenders.
3. 26 June: Rommel attacks Marsa Matrûh–Sidi Hamza Line. Auchinleck orders Eighth Army to withdraw to Alamein Line.
4. 30 June: Rommel reaches the Alamein Line.

Panzerarmee Afrika

Eighth

MEDITERRANEAN SEA

EGYPT

LIBYA

CYRENAICA

Qattara Depression

El Alamein
Fuka
Marsa Matrûh
Charing Cross
Sidi Hamza
Sidi Barrani
Menastir
Bardia
Sollum
Halfaya Pas
Siwa
Jarabub
Tobruk
Knightsbridge
El Adem
Bir el Gubi
Gazala
Bir Hakeim

British Eighth Army defence line
A Gazala Line
B Marsa Matrûh– Sidi Hamza Line
C El Alamein Line

N

0   50 miles
0   100km

9

entry into the war. Rommel, on the other hand, had withdrawn his forces intact and was reinforced early in 1942 by 90th Light Division, ready to resume the offensive. Axis forces attacked eastwards once again on 21 January and pushed the British back to a prepared line running south from Gazala.

From early February until mid May there was a lull in the fighting while the two sides built up their forces in preparation for a renewed offensive. Rommel struck first on 26 May and over the next few weeks out-fought and out-manoeuvred Ritchie's army. During the protracted struggle Eighth Army lost 50,000 men and was forced into retreat, streaming back in some disarray towards the Egyptian border. Tobruk was abandoned along with quantities of supplies and equipment. A jubilant Rommel pressed hard on the heels of the British withdrawal, intent on driving straight though to Cairo.

On 23 June the battered Eighth Army took up a position just inside Egypt at Mersa Matruh. Complete defeat became a distinct possibility. Auchinleck realized that drastic steps had to be taken to prevent the enemy reaching the Nile Delta and capturing the Suez Canal, for once Axis troops were across the waterway, Hitler might be tempted to send forces south from the Caucasus to link up with them and then move on the oil fields of Iraq and Persia.

With few features standing above the flat desert landscape, a British officer uses the height of his Marmon Herrington armoured vehicle to improve his view of the enemy. (IWM E14068)

Auchinleck at this point removed Ritchie and placed himself in personal command of Eighth Army. His overriding consideration was to keep the army intact, even if it meant giving up Egypt. After a two-day running battle at Mursa Matruh, the withdrawal continued to a half-prepared defensive line at El Alamein. To the rear of this, just before the delta, he ordered more defences to be dug and asked his planners to consider how further withdrawals into Palestine or south towards the Sudan could be effected. Auchinleck planned to stop Rommel's advance at El Alamein. Failing that, he would try again on a makeshift line before the Delta. Whatever happened, he would not allow Eight Army to be overwhelmed; it must be kept intact as a fighting force to continue the struggle with the enemy, wherever the next battlefield might happen to be.

British Eighth Army, exhausted by its hurried retreat, was in position on the El Alamein line by 30 June. Following close behind, the equally weary advance units of Rommel's Panzerarmee Afrika brushed up against it the same day. Both sides now squared up to each other across kilometres of barren desert and quickly prepared for a decisive showdown: one aiming for victory, the other merely trying to stop the rot. The fighting that followed, however, did not end in a decisive showdown, for it took three separate battles before a result could be declared.

The first of these battles is usually recognized as being First Alamein, although many modern historians take exception to this title, believing that Gen Auchinleck's successful attempt to stop Rommel was no more than two weeks of disparate actions fought by two exhausted armies each trying to regain the upper hand. The second battle was Alam Halfa, Rommel's last, unsuccessful operation to get past a revitalized Eighth Army into Egypt. By then things had changed; Auchinleck had gone, replaced by Gen Harold Alexander, and Eighth Army had a new commander, LtGen Bernard Montgomery. Alam Halfa marked the beginning of the turnaround in British fortunes: Rommel was stopped and the initiative passed to Montgomery. Then, after both sides had spent almost two months in preparation, came the battle known to the world as El Alamein: Montgomery's greatest triumph, when Rommel was finally defeated in a stand-up fight.

CHRONOLOGY

1942

26 May Rommel attacks British line at Gazala and, after a long, drawn-out battle, breaks through Gen Ritchie's Eighth Army.

14 June A general retreat by Eighth Army to the Marsa Matruh–Sidi Hamza line is ordered. The 2nd South African Division is left to hold Tobruk.

21 June Tobruk falls.

25 June Auchinleck removes Ritchie and takes over direct command of Eighth Army.

26 June Auchinleck cancels his order for a stand on the Marsa Matruh–Sidi Hamza line and instructs his formations to fall back to the El Alamein line, but the enemy is already in contact and a two-day battle of disengagement is fought by the almost-surrounded British X and XIII Corps.

30 June All British forces are withdrawn behind the Alamein positions.

1–3 July Rommel launches an infantry attack against the Alamein 'box' with 90th Light Division and sends his Afrika Korps round its flank. Both attacks fail to dislodge the British.

9 July Rommel attacks in the south of the line with the tanks of 21st Panzer and Littorio Divisions, but fails to make a breakthrough.

10–14 July Australian 9th Division captures Tel el Eisa near the coast and withstands counterattacks against both this salient and the Alamein 'box'.

15–17 July New Zealand Division launches an unsuccessful attack on the Ruweisat Ridge, failing to dislodge the enemy.

21–22 July Combined Australian, New Zealand and South African attack on Rommel's centre is initially successful. However, further countermoves by the enemy eventually drive them back.

26–27 July The Australians begin an attack south-westwards from Tel el Eisa towards the Miteirya Ridge. By this time both sides are well established in defence and tired. The Australian attack fails to shift the enemy and Auchinleck calls a halt. Both he and Rommel realize that further gains are impossible before their forces have rested and replenished their supplies. Both now strengthen their defences and gather for the next attack. This first battle of Alamein has stopped Rommel's advance towards Cairo and saved Egypt.

12 August Montgomery arrives in Egypt to take over Eighth Army. Alexander has already assumed command as C-in-C Middle East in place of Auchinleck.

31 August Rommel launches his final attack to break through the Alamein line.

1–4 September After two days of fighting, Axis forces are unable to get past Montgomery's strong defences about Alam Halfa Ridge and Rommel pulls back his army. His retreat is then hit in the flank by the New Zealand Division, but the counterattack is beaten off with only minimal losses.

September–October Rommel continues to strengthen his defences and Montgomery carries on with the build-up of his forces ready for the showdown battle on the Alamein line.

23 October Montgomery fires the largest artillery barrage yet seen in the war and launches Operation *Lightfoot*. XXX Corps attacks the northern minefields of Rommel's positions and attempts to carve out an area ready for X Corps to force two corridors through the Axis defences.

One of the hazards of the desert, a sand storm, is rolling across the flat terrain and will soon engulf this British officer and his jeep in an impenetrable cloud of grit and choking dust. One such incident disrupted Rommel's initial attack during the first Alamein battle. (IWM E17824)

Welcome supplies, including bread and water, arrive at the *Panzerwerkstattkompanie* (tank repair company) of the 21st Panzer Division's 5th Panzer Regiment. (Bundesarchiv 1011-782-0006-22)

The arrival of Lee and Grant tanks in the desert at last gave the British weapons that could take on the German Panzer IVs on something like parity. The sponson-mounted 75mm gun and the turret-mounted 37mm gun gave it the kind of punch that had been missing in British armour. Illustrated here is the Lee, it differed from the Grant in having a commander's machine gun cupola on the top of the turret. (IWM E14050)

LEFT **Troops from Australian 9th Division try to master the workings of a captured Italian 47/32 M25 anti-tank gun. (IWM E16678)**

Once through the German line, Monty intends to bring the German armour to battle on his terms. Secondary attacks are also launched in the south by XIII Corps to confuse the enemy.

24–26 October Montgomery's corps in both sectors of the line fail to penetrate the main German defences. In the north the armour of British X Corps is reluctant to advance too far forward of the infantry. Constant urgings by Montgomery fail to galvanize his forces for a supreme effort.

26 October Australian 9th Division begins to carve out a salient around Point 29 in the north and 1st Armoured Division attack Kidney Ridge to the south of the Australian effort.

27 October Rommel launches a counterattack against 1st Armoured Division with his Afrika Korps, but is checked by the British division's anti-tank guns. Similar enemy attacks against the Australians are also turned back.

28–30 October Montgomery now switches his main effort to the north and uses the Australian Division to carve out a salient towards the coast. Rommel counters this move by shifting more of his armour northwards.

Italian infantry with their standard infantry anti-tank gun, the 47/32 M35. This gun was built under licence and derived from the Austrian 47mm Böhler gun. No shield was provided as the gun could be broken down into five loads for easy transportation. Its low profile made it difficult to detect in the desert. (IWM RML 627)

1 November Montgomery changes his plans again and decides to throw his main weight into the line south of the Australians in Operation *Supercharge*.

2 November The New Zealand infantry attack on a two-brigade front and break into the German defences. Superb fighting by 9th Armoured Brigade holds open a gap to allow the armour of X Corps to pass through.

3 November A battle of attrition grinds down the enemy defences and they begin to crumble. Cracks open in the line and more and more of Eighth Army's divisions begin to fight their way through.

4 November The Battle of Alamein is won. Axis forces are in retreat, streaming back towards the coast road, heading for the Egyptian border.

8 November Anglo-American forces under Gen Eisenhower land in Morocco and Algeria then move swiftly into Tunisia. Rommel now has an Allied army to his front and rear.

23 November Rommel is back where he started in January 1942 at El Agheila. He plans to make a stand, but then slips away as the British try to outflank his lines. Panzerarmee Afrika is now in full retreat westwards, intending to make a stand on the Mareth Line inside Tunisia.

OPPOSING COMMANDERS

Gen Sir Claude Auchinleck C-in-C Middle East (left), talking to LtGen Neil Ritchie, Commander Eighth Army, during the ill-fated Gazala battle in May 1942. (IWM 13801)

Senior commanders of XXX Corps in discussion about the forthcoming battle. From left to right, LtGen Morshead (Australian 9th Division), LtGen Wimberley (51st Highland Division, LtGen Leese (XXX Corps) and MajGen Pienaar (South African 1st Division). (IWM 17427)

The North African desert was a graveyard of the reputations of many senior British generals, as each in turned failed to bring about a resolute victory. It was the only ground on which Britain was in contact with Axis forces and to this battlefield were sent the best that Britain had to offer. It is therefore not surprising that the Prime Minister became depressed by the continued lack of success of his generals. In June 1942, after almost two years of battle, there should have been some concrete achievements to show for all the fighting, but British Forces were right back where they started and, more to the point, they were in serious trouble. On the enemy side, the array of senior commanders changed little in the Desert War. Those replacements that were sent to North Africa were usually as a result of death, injury or sickness.

BRITISH COMMANDERS

General Sir Claude Auchinleck (1884–1981) had been appointed as Commander-in-Chief Middle East in July 1941, replacing Gen Sir Archibald Wavell, who was sacked after the disastrous attempts to relieve the besieged port of Tobruk. Ulster-born Auchinleck was a product of the colonial Indian Army, having been commissioned into 62nd Punjab Regiment in 1904. He saw action in the First World War in Egypt, Aden and Mesopotamia. After the outbreak of war in 1939, he commanded the British and French troops in northern Norway during the abortive campaign of 1940 and later took up corps and army commands in England before moving east to become C-in-C India. As C-in-C Middle East, Auchinleck had responsibility not only for military events in North Africa, but for the continuing troubles in Palestine, Iraq and Persia. He was a modest man, austere and spartan in his lifestyle, but with a great regard for the welfare of the soldiers in his command. Auchinleck was much admired by his contemporaries and proved himself an able commander when, as head of Eighth Army, he stopped Rommel's headlong charge towards Cairo at First Alamein. Unfortunately, he was not a great communicator and often irritated Churchill with his preoccupation of trying to beat Rommel rather than attending to the Prime Minister's urgings.

By August 1942, Churchill was so unhappy with Auchinleck's performance that he insisted in changes of command being made. Auchinleck was dismissed and replaced by two men: Gen Alexander as C-in-C Middle East and LtGen Montgomery as commander Eighth Army.

General Sir Harold Alexander was born the third son of the Earl of Caledon and was educated at Harrow. He graduated from Sandhurst in 1911 and gained a commission in the Irish Guards. He saw service in the First World War as a battalion commander, during which time he was twice wounded and won both the MC and DSO. Between the wars he served in India and in 1937 at the age of 45 became the youngest major-general in the British Army. He commanded 1st Division in France in 1940 and then I Corps during the evacuation at Dunkirk. He then served in Burma before taking over in the Middle East. Alexander was not recognized as a commander of great strategic ability, but he was a good administrator and diplomat. He had a reputation for surrounding himself with good staff officers of great competence. In North Africa he was more than pleased to leave all strategic and tactical decisions to his army commander.

LtGen Sir Bernard Montgomery (centre) with two of his corps commanders. On the left is LtGen Oliver Leese (XXX Corps) and on the right LtGen Herbert Lumsden (X Corps). (IWM E18416)

LtGen Sir Bernard Montgomery was a thoroughly professional soldier who had made a careful study of his craft in order to develop definite ideas of how war should be conducted. He was born in 1887, the son of a bishop. He left Sandhurst in 1908 and joined the Warwickshire Regiment on the North-West Frontier of India. During the First World War he joined the BEF just after the retreat from Mons in August 1914. He was wounded two months later and awarded the DSO. He ended the war as Chief-of Staff of 47th Division. In the inter-war years he became an instructor at Camberley. At the outbreak of the Second World War he was in command of 3rd Division. He took this formation to France in 1940 and then assumed command of II Corps on the retreat to Dunkirk. For the next two years he rose in rank until he eventually led South-Eastern Army. Montgomery had no doubts about his own ability and was contemptuous of the lack of proficiency in others. He was a difficult man to work for, or to be in command of, and had a number of detractors amongst his fellow officers. Many found him insufferable, but few doubted his competence.

After he had taken over Eighth Army in August 1942, Montgomery sought to replace some of his subordinate commanders with men that he knew. His judgement was usually proved right and many of these men themselves went on to higher command. **LtGen Sir Oliver Leese,** a tank specialist who had instructed at the Quetta Staff College in the 1930s, was brought out to Egypt from the Guards Division to lead XXX Corps. His performance in the desert eventually led to him taking over command of Eighth Army later in the war in Italy. Sometimes Montgomery was wrong in his choice of subordinates as in the case of **LtGen Herbert Lumsden** who was given the command of X Corps. Lumsden had previously commanded 1st Armoured Division and was elevated to corps command on the recommendation of others. X Corps did not perform well during the main battle of El Alamein, where Lumsden and his armoured commanders disagreed with the army commander's use of armour. Montgomery was not best pleased and replaced Lumsden soon after the battle.

The war in the desert produced many fine divisional commanders, the most impressive of which was **LtGen Sir Bernard Freyberg VC**, commander New Zealand 2nd Division. The bravery he showed in the First World War where he won Britain's highest decoration, continued in the desert, for the actions fought by his division won great praise, not least of which came

LtGen Brian Horrocks, Commander XIII Corps. Horrocks was highly regarded by Montgomery and the new Eighth Army commander lost no time in promoting him to corps command. XIII Corps had previously been led by LtGen 'Strafer' Gott who had been Churchill's first choice to take over Eighth Army after Auchinleck, but Gott was killed in an air crash days before he could assume the command. (IWM 16462)

LtGen Sir Bernard Freyberg (centre), commander of New Zealand 2nd Division, greets the Foreign Secretary, Sir Anthony Eden, on his visit to Egypt. (E18781)

The Desert Fox, Generalfeldmarschall Erwin Rommel, Commander *Panzerarmee Afrika*. Around his neck he wears the *Pour le Mérite* Cross that he won in the First War and the Knight's Cross of the Iron Cross with Oakleaves. He was awarded his Knight's Cross on 26 May 1940 and then became the tenth recipient of Oakleaves on 21 March 1941. Further awards followed; on 20 January 1942 he was the sixth person to be awarded Swords and on 11 March 1943 was the first non-Luftwaffe recipient of Diamonds to his Knight's Cross. (IWM GER 1281)

from Rommel himself who regarded the New Zealanders as being among the elite of the British Army. Similar regard was given to the other two commanders of Dominion divisions: **LtGen Sir Leslie Morshead** of Australian 9th Division and **MajGen D.H. Pienaar** of South African First Division.

AXIS COMMANDERS

The Axis chain of command in North Africa was rather complex. The theatre was, strictly speaking, an Italian show, with **Marshal Ugo Cavallero** as its Commando Supremo. Cavallero was a veteran of the First World War who had spent a great deal of time in the inter-war years in industry. He was C-in-C East Africa before succeeding Marshal Badoglio as Italian Chief of General Staff in November 1940. Marshal Cavallero reported directly to the Fascist leader Benito Mussolini in Rome. Also in Italy was the veteran Luftwaffe commander **Generalfeldmarschall Albert Kesselring** who was C-in-C of all German forces in the Mediterranean. German and Italian forces in North Africa had been combined, with the overall commander of these troops being **Marshal Ettore Bastico**. The reality was, however, that GFM Erwin Rommel commanded the actual fighting troops. Bastico had fallen out with Rommel over the strategy for retaking Tobruk in 1941 and remained hostile to the German commander for the rest of the campaign. In practice then, the Germans had taken over the running of the campaign and Rommel received his orders direct from the OKW in Berlin. The set-up was frustrating for Rommel, for most of the decisions regarding the crucial provision of supplies, shipping and transport were still controlled by the Italians and were not under his direct command. Throughout the campaign Rommel was to be plagued by these supply problems to such an extent that they had great influence on the outcome of several actions.

Generalfeldmarschall Erwin Rommel (1891–1944) had joined 6th Württemberg as an officer cadet in 1910. During the Great War he was in action in France, Romania and Italy. He was twice wounded and won the Iron Cross 1st and 2nd Class together with Germany's highest award for bravery, the *Pour le Mérite*. He later drew on his wartime experiences and wrote a book called *Infantry Tactics* which was met with great acclaim throughout Europe. Hitler was an admirer of the book and Rommel for a time commanded the Führer's security battalion. Rommel never qualified for the General Staff but still managed to achieve regular promotion during the inter-war period to reach the rank of Generalmajor in 1939. His actions in command of 7th Panzer Division in France in 1940 earned him a great reputation as an armoured commander. This reputation grew with successes in North Africa after he had taken over Axis armoured formations in March 1941. Nicknamed the 'Desert Fox', he quickly gained almost legendary status on both sides from his use of mobile forces. His superior tactical skill saw him achieve some remarkable victories, the most spectacular of which was at Gazala in May 1942.

Three field marshals discuss the situation in Egypt. From left to right, GFM Erwin Rommel (Panzerarmee Afrika), GFM Albert Kesselring (German C-in-C Mediterranean) and Marshal Ugo Cavallero (Italian Commando Supremo). (Bundesarchiv 1011-786-0326-12)

Rommel visits the Afrika Korps' HQ in June 1942 to consult with some of its senior officers. From left to right, Oberst Fritz Bayerlein (Chief of Staff), Oberstleutnant Mellenthin (in charge of operations), GFM Rommel and GenLt Walther Nehring (Commander Afrika Korps). (Bundesarchiv 1011-784-0203-14A)

Rommel was made a field marshal by Hitler after his success in recapturing Tobruk in June 1942.

There were many other very able German commanders in North Africa, some of whom went on to greater things. **General der Panzertruppe Walther Nehring** led the Afrika Korps during First Alamein. He had served in the German infantry in the First World War and switched over to tanks in the 1930s. He commanded 18th Panzer Division in Russia before joining Rommel. By the end of the war he had risen to the command of First Panzer Army. After Nehring was wounded in the Alam Halfa battle, the Afrika Korps was commanded by **Generalleutnant Wilhelm Ritter von Thoma**. During the First World War he had fought with distinction and was awarded the Bavarian Order of Max-Josef and the title of Ritter. He was a professional soldier and pursued his career during the inter-war years in the Reichswehr and later in the Wehrmacht, becoming a specialist in the use of mobile forces. In Russia he had commanded both 6th and 20th Panzer Divisions.

RIGHT **GenMaj Georg von Bismarck, commander 21st Panzer Division, in front of one of his division's Panzer IIIs from 5th Panzer Regiment. Von Bismarck was killed by British shellfire during the first day of the Alam Halfa battle on 1 September 1942.** (Bundesarchiv 1011-784-0231-35)

FAR, RIGHT **Gen Giuseppe de Stefanis, commander Italian XX Corps. De Stefanis had commanded both the Trento and Ariete Divisions in North Africa before assuming corps command. During Rommel's retreat in November 1942, he was assigned the command of Commandotruppe Mareth to prepare the defences of the Mareth Line ready for Panzerarmee Afrika to withdraw into. He later commanded LI Army Corps in Italy.** (Private collection)

Many of the Italian generals who commanded formations in Panzerarmee Afrika have come in for a good deal of criticism. They are often portrayed as being weak and ineffectual. This broad sweep of censure is often unfair. Although leadership at the top was consistently poor, some of the Italian divisions fought remarkably well in adversity and their generals did the best they could with the means available. **General Giuseppe de Stefanis**, commander of Italian XX Corps was a veteran leader of combat units in the First World War. He commanded the Pinerolo Division in Greece in 1941 and had won the *Ordine Militare di Savoia*, one of Italy's highest military awards. He had led both the Trento and Ariete Divisions in North Africa before being elevated to corps command.

OPPOSITE **Gen Francesco Arena, Commander Italian Ariete Armoured Division. Gen Arena took command of the division in May 1942 and was later awarded the Ritterkreuz by Rommel after Alamein. Following the collapse of Axis forces in Africa, he commanded the Forli Infantry Division in Greece and then became a prisoner of war to the Germans when Italy pulled out of the conflict. He escaped from a POW camp in January 1945, but was unfortunately shot dead by a Russian patrol.** (Private collection)

OPPOSING ARMIES

There is no doubt that at the end of June 1942, when Eighth Army had been forced back into Egypt and Rommel's army was in close pursuit, Auchinleck's forces were at a very low ebb. The strength that had been built up over the previous six months for the final offensive to push Rommel out of Africa had been squandered in a poorly fought battle at Gazala against an army commander who was a master of mobile tactics. The Gazala action and those skirmishes that followed did not, however, constitute a complete rout. Auchinleck had all the while kept his army in existence. Although much of his force was strung out across the desert and thoroughly disorganized, he still had confidence that he would be able to pull it together and face the enemy for what could be its final battle.

BRITISH FORCES

Early in 1942 Eighth Army had been forced to provide formations for the fighting in the Far East and it took time for new divisions and supplies to be shipped out from the UK to gradually build it back to full strength. Much of this new strength had been lost at Gazala, but Eight Army still remained a potent force when Rommel entered Egypt. The composition of Auchinleck's army during First Alamein was a mix of infantry and armoured formations from Britain and its Dominions. Many of these divisions, such as 7th Armoured Division (the Desert Rats), were veterans

British 6-pdr anti-tank gun in action. The arrival of the 6-pdr in North Africa in mid-1942 gave the British a powerful weapon with which to finally counter German tanks. Its 2.84kg shell could penetrate 50mm of armour at 1,500 metres. (IWM E15559)

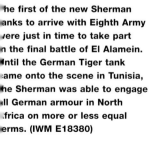

Early model American Stuart light tank in British service with riveted hull. The tank is from 4th Armoured Division and its crew are looking towards the high ground of Qaret el Himeimat. (IWM E16095)

of the fighting in North Africa with a long list of battle honours to their name. Others were newly arrived on the continent. There was a large contingent of divisions from the countries of the old British Empire, with formations arriving from New Zealand, Australia, South Africa and India. These were especially welcome for Britain struggling to raise enough equipped divisions for service on three continents, for these formations had a reputation for being aggressive in attack and dogged in defence. They were all well regarded by friend and foe alike.

In late June 1942, there were three corps in Eighth Army: X, XIII and XXX Corps. HQ X Corps, however, had arrived from Syria on 21 June, too late to have any part in stemming the German onslaught. During the first action at Alamein it remained in the delta. When Montgomery arrived in Egypt he decided to reconstitute this formation with armoured divisions as a mobile corps along the lines of the Afrika Korps. The other two corps fought in all three of the Alamein battles, with both armoured and infantry divisions under command.

Reinforcements for British units continued to arrive in North Africa in regular quantities which kept all formations up to near their nominal strength. Even so, there were times, especially after stiff actions, when numbers in the division fell to levels which required the unit to be pulled out of the line for rest and replenishment. Casualties were more of a problem for the Dominion divisions. Their replacements had to come from their own national reserves. This made losses in action keenly felt back home, which in turn created some disquiet among their politicians. Also bolstering British forces were contingents of troops from other European countries. The 1st Greek Brigade was used to hold defensive positions in the line, and 1st and 2nd Free French Brigades

The first of the new Sherman tanks to arrive with Eighth Army were just in time to take part in the final battle of El Alamein. Until the German Tiger tank came onto the scene in Tunisia, the Sherman was able to engage all German armour in North Africa on more or less equal terms. (IWM E18380)

were committed to secondary attacks on the edge of the Qattara Depression during the final battle at Alamein.

British and Commonwealth divisions were organized along similar lines. Infantry divisions contained three infantry brigades each with three rifle battalions, a reconnaissance regiment, a machine-gun battalion and three field and one anti-tank regiments of artillery. Armoured Divisions comprised one armoured and one motorized infantry brigade with two field and one anti-tank regiments of guns. Each armoured brigade contained three armoured regiments and one motor battalion. Up until First Alamein the artillery was distributed among brigades. Auchinleck changed this so that all of the guns were centralized under the command of Divisional HQ. This change was formalized for all divisions in August 1942.

While training and support for Eighth Army was quite adequate, weapons and equipment were often below the standards of the Germans. One of the great problems was in British tank design which, up until that time in the war, had not been very successful. They were often easily outperformed by German models. Crusader and Valentine tanks were the most numerous in the desert and both were armed with small 2-pdr (40mm) weapons, although some later-version Crusader IIIs with 6-pdr (57mm) guns were beginning to arrive in Egypt. The Crusader also had a reputation for being unreliable. Things improved somewhat with the arrival of the American-built Grant tank for this was armed with both a large 75mm gun and a 37mm weapon which could engage German tanks on something like an equal footing, but the tank had its disadvantages. Its main gun was sponson-mounted on its side and had a very limited traverse. Its three-metre high profile also towered over the battlefield making it very difficult for it to be concealed in the open desert. Just before Montgomery's final battle at El Alamein, American Sherman tanks began to arrive in the theatre. These had a turret-mounted 75mm gun, were capable of reasonably high speeds and were highly manoeuvrable. With them, the British finally had a tank that could match German armour.

The other critical problem encountered by the British was the

German Luftwaffe SdKfz 7 medium tractor pulling an 88mm flak gun to be used in an anti-tank role. The gun already has a number of 'kills' to its credit as shown by the rings around its barrel near the muzzle. (IWM MH5833)

inadequacy of its main anti-tank gun, the 2-pdr (40mm). It just did not have enough punch to stop enemy tanks at anything like the distance they should be engaged. Fortunately, a new anti-tank gun, the 6-pdr (57mm), was beginning to arrive in Egypt in large numbers. This was a much more potent weapon and was quickly used to re-arm the anti-tank regiments of the Royal Artillery and then the anti-tank companies of the infantry battalions themselves. The sensible deployment of this type of gun curtailed Rommel's ability to charge at the British as he had done so often in the past.

One of the greatest advantages that Eighth Army had over the enemy was the support of Air Vice-Marshal Sir Arthur Coningham's Desert Air Force, flying from airstrips close to the action. During the earlier battles in Libya it was the German Luftwaffe and the Italian Regia Aeronautica that commanded the sky from their more local landing grounds. The further the Axis forces advanced into Egypt the less effective their air forces became. It was not just the long flying time to the front that put them at a disadvantage, the Desert Air Force had in the meantime gradually begun to obtain a numerical advantage over its rivals. By the time of the Alamein battles it had almost complete superiority over the enemy's air fleet and was able to bomb and strafe rear areas with such regularity that it had a marked effect on the conduct of the battles on the ground.

AXIS FORCES

Whilst Panzerarmee Afrika was not solely a German formation, its command was German, its strategy was German inspired and its tactical deployment was German led. Its main strike force was contained in the German Afrika Korps, with 15th and 21st Panzer Divisions. This crack formation was supported by the equally famous motorized 90th Light Division. A little later, in July 1942, these were joined by 164th Light 'Afrika' Division. All of these divisions were well trained, well led and highly mobile. They were the strike force of Rommel's army, but by no means his only mobile units.

At First Alamein two Italian armoured divisions (Ariete and Littorio)

Artillery crew of a German FH18 150mm field howitzer await orders to open fire. The gun could deliver a 43kg shell up to a distance of 13,325 metres. It became the standard German heavy field howitzer of the war. (Bundesarchiv 1011-783-0119-17A)

GFM Rommel inspects a knocked-out Stuart tank belonging to the headquarters of a British armoured battalion. (IWM MH5875)

An Italian M13/40 tank being unloaded from a transporter. The tank was slow, uncomfortable and under-powered, but still served as the basic armoured vehicle in all of the Italian armoured units. Its 47mm gun, however, was accurate and its armour-piercing capability was superior to the British Crusader and Valentine tanks which were armed with the 2-pdr gun. (Ufficio Storico Esercito Rome)

and one motorized division (Trieste) were with Rommel, combined in Italian XX Corps. None of these divisions were quite as competent or as skilful as their German counterparts for they were let down by the ineffectiveness of their armour. They were, none the less, a vital link in Rommel's mobile tactics. The often maligned Italian infantry divisions with Panzerarmee Afrika were also indispensable. The Trento, Sabratha, Bologna, Brescia and Pavia Divisions grouped in X and XXI Corps were not as proficient as German formations, but could put up an effective fight when suitably led and deployed. They were used to hold the line, occupy territory and man fixed defences for just long enough to allow the armoured divisions to intervene. In some ways they were seen as 'cannon fodder', there to absorb the shock of any major attack. Such cynical use dispirited their commanders and affected morale in the ranks. Most Italian troops simply wished for a speedy end to the war so that they could all return home, their dreams of African conquests replaced by a determination to survive.

The Italian Army was inadequately served by its weapons. Its main tanks, the M13/40 and the M14/41 variant, were the poorest in Africa in terms of armament, armour protection and performance and its 47/32 M35 anti-tank gun had less penetrative power than the British 2-pdr gun. The same was not true of the equipment in the German arsenal, for it contained two very prominent weapons, the Panzer IV Special and the 88mm gun, that outperformed all else on the battlefield. The Panzer IV tank was the best of the German armour and it was further improved in the summer of 1942 by the introduction of a new longer-barrelled 75mm gun to become Panzer IVF2 with almost twice the penetrative power of its predecessor. It was true that not many of these tanks were available to Rommel during his initial move into Egypt, but when they did put in an appearance, they proved to be extremely effective. The 88mm gun was strictly speaking an anti-aircraft weapon, but when used in an anti-tank role it proved to be irresistible. The flat trajectory and high velocity of its shells outclassed every other weapon on the battlefield. Its one drawback was its high profile; it stood very tall in the open desert.

The two armoured divisions of the Afrika Korps both consisted of one Panzer and one Panzergrenadier regiments. The Italian armoured divisions were likewise configured with one tank regiment and one motorized infantry regiment. The German 90th and 164th Divisions had three motorized infantry regiments. Italian motorized and infantry divisions each contained just two regiments.

Rommel's problems were not confined to just countering the British, he also had to contend with the battle for supplies. The provision of vehicles, reinforcements, weapons and fuel were Panzerarmee Afrika's greatest worry. With the battered ports of Tripoli and Benghazi located hundreds of kilometres in the rear, the long trek to obtain sufficient quantities of supplies forwards into Egypt was a constant headache for Rommel. Everything required for battle had to be shipped across the Mediterranean Sea. There were often sufficient stores and transport available in Italy, but each ship bringing goods across to North Africa had to run the gauntlet of naval and air attacks from British forces based in Malta and Egypt. In July 1942 only 20 per cent of the required total was unloaded in Libya, whilst in August Rommel's army used up twice the amount that was landed. All stocks were running perilously low and the scarcity of fuel especially had a great influence on the shape of the battles fought in the summer of 1942.

ORDER OF BATTLE: BRITISH FORCES

Commander-in-Chief Middle East – Gen the Hon Sir Harold Alexander

British Eighth Army – LtGen Sir Bernard Montgomery

Army Troops
　　1st Anti-tank Brigade
　　1st Armoured Brigade
　　2nd Anti-aircraft Brigade
　　12th Anti-aircraft Brigade
　　21st Independent Infantry Brigade

X Corps – LtGen Herbert Lumsden

1st Armoured Division – MajGen R. Briggs
　　2nd Armoured Brigade
　　7th Motorized Brigade
　　Hammerforce (From 8th Armoured Division)

8th Armoured Division – MajGen C.H. Gairdner
　　24th Armoured Brigade (To 10th Armoured Division)
　　Hammerforce (To 1st Armoured Division)

10th Armoured Division – MajGen A.H. Gatehouse
　　8th Armoured Brigade
　　24th Armoured Brigade (From 8th Armoured Division)
　　133rd Lorried Infantry Brigade (From 44th Division)

XIII Corps – LtGen Brian Horrocks

7th Armoured Division – MajGen A.F. Harding
　　4th Light Armoured Brigade
　　22nd Armoured Brigade
　　1st Free French Brigade Group

44th Division – MajGen I.T.P. Hughes
　　131st Brigade
　　132nd Brigade
　　133rd Brigade (To 10th Armoured Division)

50th Division – MajGen J.S. Nichols
　　69th Infantry Brigade
　　151st Infantry Brigade
　　1st Greek Brigade

　　2nd Free French Brigade Group
XXX Corps – LtGen Sir Oliver Leese

23rd Armoured Brigade Group (Corps Reserve)

Indian 4th Division – MajGen F.I.S. Tuker
　　5th Indian Brigade
　　7th Indian Brigade
　　161st Indian Brigade

51st (Highland) Division – MajGen D.N. Wimberley
　　152nd Brigade
　　153rd Brigade
　　154th Brigade

Australian 9th Division – LtGen Sir Leslie Morshead
　　20th Australian Brigade
　　24th Australian Brigade
　　26th Australian Brigade

New Zealand 2nd Division – LtGen Sir Bernard Freyberg VC
　　5th New Zealand Brigade
　　6th New Zealand Brigade
　　9th Armoured Brigade

South African 1st Division MajGen D.H. Pienaar
　　1st South African Brigade
　　2nd South African Brigade
　　3rd South African Brigade

Troops of the South African 1st Division together with their Marmon Herrington armoured cars captured by Germans after the Gazala battles. (Bundesarchiv 1011-784-0232-22A)

German cans, called 'jerrycans' by the British, are being filled with water ready for transportation up to the forward positions. The prominent white crosses painted on the containers distinguish them from cans carrying petrol. (Bundesarchiv 1011-782-0033-16A)

Panzer IV with short-barrel 75mm gun from 8th Panzer Regiment of 15th Panzer Division. Its triangular divisional sign can be seen to the right of the driver's slit. (Bundesarchiv 1011-439-1276-12)

ORDER OF BATTLE: AXIS FORCES

Italian Commando Supremo – Benito Mussolini
    Chief of Staff – Marshal Count Ugo Cavallero

German Commander-in-Chief South – GFM Albert Kesselring

Italian Commando Supremo Africa – Marshal Ettore Bastico

Panzerarmee Afrika – GFM Erwin Rommel

ITALIAN FORCES

Italian X Corps – Gen Enrico Frattini (acting)

9th Regt Bersaglieri

17th Divisione di Fanteria 'Pavia' – Gen Nazareno Scattaglia
    27th Regt Fanteria
    28th Regt Fanteria

27th Divisione di Fanteria 'Brescia' – Gen Brunetto Brunetti
    19th Regt Fanteria
    20th Regt Fanteria

185th Divisione Paracadutisti 'Folgore' – Gen Enrico Frattini
    186th Regt Paracadutisti
    187th Regt Paracadutisti
    Raggruppamento 'Ruspoli' (Battle Group)

Italian XX Corps – Gen Giuseppe De Stefanis

101st Divisione Motorizzata 'Trieste' – Gen Francesco La Ferla
    65th Regt Fanteria Motorizzata
    66th Regt Fanteria Motorizzata
    VIII Battaglione Bersaglieri
    XI Battaglione Corazzato

132nd Divisione Corazzata 'Ariete' – Gen Francesco Arena
    132nd Regt Corazzato
    8th Regt Bersaglieri
    III Gruppo Squadroni 'Nizza Cavalleria'

133rd Divisione Corazzata 'Littorio' – Gen Gervasio Bitossi
    133rd Regt Corazzato
    12th Regt Bersaglieri
    III Gruppo Squadroni 'Lanceri de Novaria'

Italian XXI Corps – Gen Alessandro Gloria (acting)

7th Regt Bersaglieri

25th Divisione di Fanteria 'Bologna' – Gen Alessandro Gloria
    39th Regt Fanteria
    40th Regt Fanteria

102nd Divisione di Fanteria 'Trento' – Gen Giorgio Masina
    61st Regt Fanteria

62nd Regt Fanteria
Italian Reserve (still forming)

136th Divisione Corazzata 'Giovani Fascisti' – Gen Ismaele di Nisio
    Regt Fanteria 'Giovani Fascisti'
    III Gruppo Squadroni 'Cavalleggeri di Monferrato'

GERMAN FORCES

90th Leichte Division – GenLt Theodor Graf von Sponeck
    155th Regiment
    200th Regiment
    361st Motorized Regiment

164th Leichte 'Afrika' Division – GenMaj Carl-Hans Lungershausen
    125th Panzergrenadier Regiment
    382nd Panzergrenadier Regiment
    433rd Panzergrenadier Regiment

Ramcke Parachute Brigade – GenMaj Hermann-Bernhard Ramcke

Deutsches Afrika Korps – GenLt Wilhelm Ritter von Thoma

15th Panzer Division – GenMaj Gustav von Vaerst
    8th Panzer Regiment
    115th Panzergrenadier Regiment

21st Panzer Division – GenMaj Heinz von Randow
    5th Panzer Regiment
    104th Panzergrenadier Regiment

OPPOSING PLANS

At the end of June 1942, when Gen Auchinleck's forces had been forced right back inside Egypt after suffering great losses in men and *matériel*, defeat was a distinct possibility. In contrast, Rommel's Panzerarmee Afrika was brimful of confidence after weeks of success, it had the smell of victory in its nostrils and was on the point of driving the British out of Egypt. At least, that is how it appeared to those who were there and to governments overseas. This appreciation was, however, flawed. The British had actually fallen back into a defendable position and could call on fresh troops previously withdrawn from the action. Other divisions were also at that moment en route for Egypt. Their lines of communication had shortened and reinforcements, tanks, fuel and new equipment were still arriving in the ports just 120 kilometres to their rear. In contrast, Rommel's forces were all exhausted. Their petrol supplies had almost dried up; their tank numbers had dwindled through breakdowns and losses; supply lines snaked back for hundreds of kilometres across the desert to bomb-damaged ports in their rear and they were short of reinforcements, fuel, tanks, transport and guns. On paper at least, it looked as though Rommel could not go on. His superiors, Kesselring, Cavallero and Bastico, all agreed that he had overextended himself; all originally urged him to stop. He would have none of it; the Nile Delta seemed there for the taking.

The British had been brought to this unenviable position by a tactically superior enemy. Rommel's reputation rested on his use of his mobile forces. When he arrived just short of Alamein on 29 June he believed he had the British on the run. It was therefore essential that he kept up the momentum; to delay would be fatal. He knew that he would have to force the Alamein line and relied on his momentum to take him through. He could not afford to wait for his exhausted force to gather strength and let his supply lines catch up with him, for the British would also use the time to rest and improve their defences. Rommel saw the Alamein position as another line on which to employ his usual tactics of a frontal assault by infantry and a wide sweep by the Afrika Korps to move behind the defenders, a plan that had worked so well in the past.

Auchinleck also stuck to the strategy he had used before. He would fight Rommel on this new defence line and, whatever happened, he would keep Eighth Army intact. If he was forced into another retreat then he would pull back to the next position already hurriedly being prepared in front of the delta in his rear. In the meantime he would fight a battle at Alamein. Tactically he would use the same plan as Rommel but in reverse. He could not man the whole of the line, so he would put strong positions of infantry and guns in 'boxes' in and around selected features, blocking the route, and then attack any penetrations between them with mobile groups. As Rommel manoeuvred to

Group of German officers from the Afrika Korps waiting for the start of an attack. (Bundesarchiv 1011-782-0023-09A)

find an opening, Auchinleck would manoeuvre to pre-vent it. It was a good plan, for it worked.

Rommel's dash for the delta was halted in a battle that was to become known as First Alamein. Auchinleck then proceeded to construct a thick line of defences to deal with the next Axis attack, paying special attention to the northern sector which he had extensively mined in an effort to force Rommel to consider attacking in the south, past the long Alam Halfa Ridge. Auchinleck rightly determined that this ridge would be the key to the next battle, for Rommel would have to either pass alongside it or manoeuvre round it. Either way, Auchinleck intended to be ready for him. Then things changed; Churchill urged Auchinleck to go back on the offensive while Rommel gathered strength for his next push for the Suez Canal, but Auchinleck insisted on more time. Churchill would not agree on any further delay and Auchinleck was replaced by LtGen Bernard Montgomery. Exasperatingly for Churchill, Montgomery also decided he would not go over to the offensive straight away. He would wait until he had seen off Rommel's next attempt at a breakthrough. Once Rommel had been halted, he would put in his attack, but even then he would not make his move until he had overwhelming superiority in men and weapons, and not before Eighth Army had reached a standard of training that met with his own high ideals.

Auchinleck had evolved certain tactics for defensive action in the desert. He realized that the wide featureless terrain made static positions alone ineffective – they could be easily outflanked. It was important to be able to move and concentrate against the point of enemy penetration and to bring upon him the greatest amount of firepower that was available. It was also pointless to have too many infantry in defensive positions, but those that were there needed to have sufficient anti-tank and artillery to provide an all-round defence. There also had to be an overall balance between those troops and artillery holding the line and those that were committed to a mobile role. Units and headquarters in the immediate rear had to be prepared to defend themselves in the event that the enemy managed to break through the forward positions and overrun them. They also had to be able to hold out until mobile forces were able to help clear away the enemy. This doctrine led to the arrangement of defence localities termed 'boxes', which usually contained two battalions of infantry, and a battery each of field, anti-aircraft and anti-tank guns. The remainder of the division was organized into mobile groups.

Montgomery did not like the idea of boxes. He thought that divisions should fight as divisions with all their artillery massed in support. He also took note from Rommel and created a mobile corps of his own, modelled along similar lines to the Afrika Korps, to be held in reserve and used as a strike force. He planned to continue Auchinleck's work to heavily fortify the northern sector of the line to a point where Rommel could only realistically make his attack in the south.

A near miss as a mine explodes close by some British transport, although this is probably a staged incident laid on for the photographers. (IWM E18542)

German soldier attempting to dig a 'foxhole' in the stony desert. With little natural cover, it was important to get below ground as soon as possible for safety. (IWM MH5834)

German signals post near Tel el Eisa. The flat featureless terrain made it possible to transmit (and listen to) radio traffic over large distances. The Germans gained much important intelligence by listening to the insecure chatter of British units talking to each other in plain language. (IWM MH 5581)

Montgomery would then mass his guns and assemble his armour to meet him, just as Auchinleck had intended.

It has to be noted that both Montgomery and Auchinleck were helped in making this decision by the use of ULTRA intercepts. The breaking of the German codes allowed both of these commanders to have an insight into Axis thinking. Such gathering of intelligence was not, however, all one-sided for the Germans were also receiving a wealth of information about British forces from two individual sources. The most important was from their own specialist listening service located in the desert, which was picking up and analysing insecure radio chatter emanating from Eighth Army. It was amazing just what could be deduced from units talking to each other over the air. More valuable news, possibly much more valuable at a higher level, was obtained by deciphering dispatches sent to Washington by Col Bonner Fellers, the US military attaché in Cairo. The Italians and Germans were both able to decipher American codes from the 'Black Book' encryption that Fellers used. The nightly dispatches radioed to the USA after he had visited British formations and talked with senior commanders was decoded by the enemy before morning. When America entered the war Fellers had privileged access to the most sensitive of information and all of this fell into German hands. The Germans later admitted that the information unwittingly supplied by Fellers contributed decisively to their victories in North Africa.

Rommel's last attack was emphatically turned back in the battle of Alam Halfa and hopes for a renewed push to the delta faded forever. Rommel knew that it was now the turn of the British to make their attack. All he could do was strengthen his defences and make ready to deal with the onslaught when it came. His plan rested on having defences of such thickness and depth that they were capable of holding the enemy back. In the event of a British penetration, his mobile armoured forces would then advance to seal it off. To counter this, Montgomery could only use brute force and overwhelming numbers. He knew that he would have to attack very strong positions and would take large numbers of casualties. The battle of attrition which would follow would have to be endured long enough for gaps to be opened for the tanks to pass through and be ready to meet with the Axis armour which would inevitably come at them. Then it would be down to a dog fight to see who was the strongest.

FIRST ALAMEIN

The El Alamein line into which Eighth Army retreated in late June was a defence line in name only. Very little had been done to prepare the ground in terms of field fortifications; its main strength was its natural location. The line stretched north to south across 65 kilometres of desert over several low ridges and shallow depressions. Anchoring the northern flank was the sea. In the south was the Qattara Depression, a massive area of soft sand and salt marsh, impassable to tanks and most kinds of transport. The Alamein line could not therefore be outflanked; Rommel would have to come through it. Attempting to block his way were three defended localities about 25 kilometres apart, the first around the railway station at El Alamein, the second in the middle of the line about Bab el Qattara and the third close to the great depression at Naqb Abu. None of these localities had been properly wired or mined.

The original German plan was for Axis forces to pause for six weeks for resupply after the capture of Tobruk, but the collapse of the British forces after Gazala led to approval being given to Rommel to advance straight into Egypt. On 28 June, after some initial reluctance on the part of senior commanders in the Mediterranean, he received specific orders to defeat the forces opposing him, seize the Suez Canal between Ismailia and Port Said, occupy Cairo and eradicate any possible threat from Alexandria. Cairo lay just 160 kilometres away and Rommel knew that if he paused he would be giving Auchinleck time to reorganize. Delay

The isolated railway station of El Alamein gave its name to the famous battle which was fought in the desert to the south. In 1942 there were just a few buildings clustered round the station, tens of miles from any other habitation. (IWM E14398)

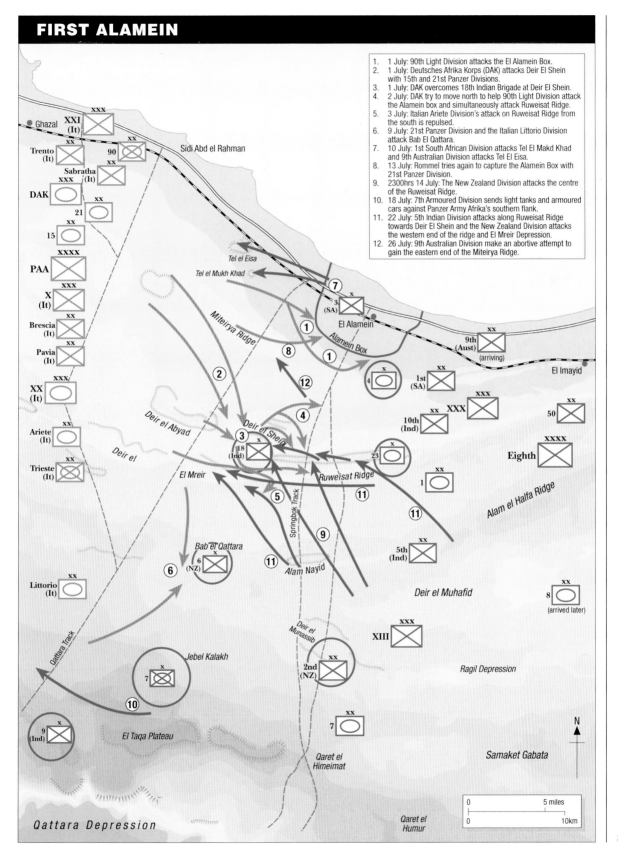

1. 1 July: 90th Light Division attacks the El Alamein Box.
2. 1 July: Deutsches Afrika Korps (DAK) attacks Deir El Shein with 15th and 21st Panzer Divisions.
3. 1 July: DAK overcomes 18th Indian Brigade at Deir El Shein.
4. 2 July: DAK try to move north to help 90th Light Division attack the Alamein box and simultaneously attack Ruweisat Ridge.
5. 3 July: Italian Ariete Division's attack on Ruweisat Ridge from the south is repulsed.
6. 9 July: 21st Panzer Division and the Italian Littorio Division attack Bab El Qattara.
7. 10 July: 1st South African Division attacks Tel El Makd Khad and 9th Australian Division attacks Tel El Eisa.
8. 13 July: Rommel tries again to capture the Alamein Box with 21st Panzer Division.
9. 2300hrs 14 July: The New Zealand Division attacks the centre of the Ruweisat Ridge.
10. 18 July: 7th Armoured Division sends light tanks and armoured cars against Panzer Army Afrika's southern flank.
11. 22 July: 5th Indian Division attacks along Ruweisat Ridge towards Deir El Shein and the New Zealand Division attacks the western end of the ridge and El Mreir Depression.
12. 26 July: 9th Australian Division make an abortive attempt to gain the eastern end of the Miteirya Ridge.

would be fatal. He realized that he would have to force the Alamein line without halting, even though his men were tired, his equipment was in need of repair and his supply lines stretched almost to breaking point. On 29 June, immediately after 90th Light Division had captured the Mursa Matruh position, Rommel sent the division eastwards with the armour of the Afrika Korps to make renewed contact with Eighth Army, their transport refuelled from stocks captured from the British.

In Alexandria and Cairo confusion reigned. Sympathetic Arabs began to prepare for the arrival of Rommel, openly sneering at the plight of the British. Panic set in amongst the rear areas; confidential documents were burned; elements of the Middle East Headquarters were moved to Palestine; the Mediterranean Fleet left Alexandria to disperse amongst the safer ports of Haifa and Beirut and arrangements were made to block the harbour and destroy port facilities and stores.

On 30 June Rommel had his strike force ready to attack between the Alamein position and Deir el Abyad. The 90th Light Division was on the left and his two panzer divisions abreast of it on the right. He intended to pass the armour down the southern side of the Miteirya Ridge towards the British near Ruweisat Ridge. The 90th would skirt the Alamein defences and then cut them off from the east while the Afrika Korps was swinging south to Alam Nayil to take British XIII Corps in the rear. Italian XXI Corps would come forward next and attack Alamein directly from the west. Italian XX Corps was to follow behind the panzer divisions then swing south to attack the Bab el Qattara position.

In the early hours of 1 July, 90th Light Division attacked eastwards intending to pass to the south of the El Alamein Box. In poor light and a sandstorm the leading units quickly lost their way and collided with the Alamein defences. The exhausted Panzergrenadiers soon became entangled in vicious fighting by an enemy who was better prepared than they expected him to be. It was not until early afternoon that the division was able to resume its advance. To the south the Afrika Korps fared little better. Both 15th and 21st Panzer Divisions found their approach to the start line difficult and arrived three hours late, bombed and disorganized by the Desert Air Force. When the advance finally got

The lonely figure of Gen Claude Auchinleck watches the last of his units arrive into the Alamein line after the rout suffered at Gazala and Mersa Matruh at the end of June 1942. (IWM E13882)

under way, they found that the area around Deir el Shein before the Ruweisat Ridge was held in some strength by 18th Indian Brigade. The brigade was newly arrived from Iraq and had been placed under the command of South African 1st Division. The panzers now came under heavy artillery fire from the Indians and the South African Division. This was something of a shock for Gen d.Pz Walther Nehring, commander of the Afrika Korps, for intelligence had suggested that these troops were much further to the east. Nehring felt that he had no option but to attack the position. This was no easy task and it was not until 1900hrs that evening that his panzer divisions managed to overwhelm the stiff resistance put up by 18th Indian Brigade and take Deir el Shein, losing 18 of its precious 55 tanks in the process.

Meanwhile, 90th Light Division had also had a bad afternoon. On its attempt to get around to the east of the Alamein Box it had run into terrific artillery fire from the guns of the South African Division and had gone to ground. Rommel's personal intervention was unable to get it moving again, for the army commander himself was caught in the barrage and forced to lay on the open ground with his troops for three hours. Further back, the Italians were attacking the other end of the Alamein position with little success.

While Rommel was face-down in the sand, Auchinleck was issuing orders for a counterattack. It had been a good day for Eighth Army's commander. His forces, suitably supported by the Desert Air Force, had blunted Rommel's first attempt to get past the Alamein line. He had lost the 18th Indian Brigade but had halted the Afrika Korps, and the slow collapse of the position at Deir el Shein through the resistance put up by the Indians had allowed Auchinleck to gather fresh forces to block the Germans. It was now essential that his defence should include tactical attacks to deflect Rommel's intentions.

Auchinleck ordered LtGen Norrie's XXX Corps to hold Rommel's advance while LtGen Gott's XIII Corps hit his right flank with armour. Gott was told to attack on either side of the Ruweisat Ridge towards Deir el Abyad. Now with both 90th Light Division and the Afrika Korps identified in the north, Auchinleck also decided that the defended localities of Bab el Qattara and Naqb abu Dweis could be abandoned to make his defence more compact. The New Zealand Division could be withdrawn and prepared for a mobile role, as could Indian 5th Division in the south.

The next day, 2 July, the German 90th Division failed to get moving again in the face of heavy British artillery fire. Rommel realized that he would have to shift some of his weight to the north to help the division to get eastwards along the coast road. Nehring's corps was ordered to detach some of his tanks break to give some support to the 90th Light Division.

The renewed German thrust and the British counter attack got underway simultaneously. The clash rippled across the northern part of the Alamein line. Fierce fighting, both north and south of the Ruweisat Ridge and on the ridge itself lasted until dark. Tanks of the 1st

**TANKS AND ANTI-TANK GUNS OF THE ITALIAN ARIETE
DIVISION ATTACKING SOUTH OF RUWEISAT RIDGE DURING
THE FIRST BATTLE OF EL ALAMEIN** (pages 36–37)

The main German effort on 3 July lay south of the Ruweisat
Ridge. The Afrika Korps launched an advance but soon ran
into British armour, readying themselves for their own
attack. The action was short and sharp, during which the
Afrika Korps was firmly held by 1st Armoured Division. A
little further to the south, British XIII Corps was also
beginning an advance, aiming for Deir el Shein. It soon
clashed with the Italian Ariete Division, which was putting
in its own attack to the right of the Afrika Korps. The
Italians were met with a fierce exchange of artillery which
was followed up by the infantry of the New Zealand Division.
Over 350 Italians were taken prisoner and 44 guns were
captured. The New Zealanders then manoeuvred to try cut
off the retreat of the Ariete, but found themselves engaged
by the Brescia Division of Italian X Corps in the depression
of El Mreir and had to retire. The battlescene shows M13/40
tanks of 1st Battalion of the Italian 132nd Ariete Armoured
Division advancing eastwards during the attack. The division
had performed well in the earlier Gazala and 'Knightsbridge'
battles and Rommel thought it was one of the better Italian
formations. The M13/40 tank (1) was the least effective
fighting vehicle in the desert, generally inferior to all other
tanks, but available to the Italians in relatively large
numbers - almost 2,000 were built during the war. It had a
slow cross-country performance, only able to reach speeds
of around 15 km/hour in action. It did, however, have an
accurate 47mm gun with an armour-piercing capability
superior to the under-gunned British tanks of the period
before Alamein. It was effective against infantry, but unable
to perform well against the faster and more heavily
armoured tanks of Eighth Army. The tank had a crew of four,
consisting of commander, loader, driver and radio
operator/machine-gunner. It did not have a specific gunner,
so the commander (2) also had to operate the main gun in
addition to his other duties. The Italian 47mm anti-tank gun
(3) was a useful weapon in the desert. Based on the
Austrian 4.7mm Böhler anti-tank gun, it did not have the
range of the devastating dual-purpose German 88mm gun,
but it had a much lower profile, was easier to dig in and was
often only detectable by British tank crews when it was
too late to avoid its fire. The gun did not have a shield for
protection, which exposed its crew to the effects of high-
explosive shell fire. Supporting the advance is a
self-propelled Semovente M40 75/18 assault gun (4). It
consisted of a large 75mm gun mounted on an M40 chassis
and gave the Italians unequalled fire power on the desert
floor, but its low speed and thin armour made it vulnerable
to British tanks and artillery. (Howard Gerrard)

The crew of a Panzer III from 21st Panzer Division watch the inexorable columns of vehicles of the Afrika Korps driving eastwards to the El Alamein line on 29 June 1942. (Bundesarchiv 1011-782-0016-32A)

Armoured Division were held by the anti-tank guns of the panzer divisions and Nehring's armour was corralled on the northern side of the ridge by the British artillery. The result was indecisive: Rommel's tired forces were too weak to push aside Auchinleck's troops and the British were too disorganized to completely repulse the advance. Eleven more German tanks had been lost in the action, reducing the DAK's panzer force to just 26 runners.

That night, his sleep broken by British bombing raids, Rommel decided to try again the next day to effect a breakthrough. He intended to probe the British defences to find a weak spot. The DAK was to renew its eastwards thrust while the Italian XX Corps advanced on its right flank; Italian X Corps was to hold El Mreir. Rommel knew that his men were exhausted, but reasoned that the British were also close to collapse; one big push would break the line. Auchinleck, in turn, still favoured an active defence and ordered XIII Corps to advance north-west of Deir el Shein in order to threaten the enemy's rear.

The main German effort on 3 July lay south of the Ruweisat Ridge. Early that morning the advance by the Afrika Korps ran into the British armour readying themselves for their attack. The action lasted for over an hour-and-a-half by which time the Germans had virtually reached the limit of their endurance. Rommel continued to urge his men on, but little further progress was made. The Afrika Korps was firmly held by 1st Armoured Division. Just to the south, British XIII Corps was beginning its advance on Deir el Shein when it bumped into the flanks of Italian Ariete Division who were crossing its front. An exchange of artillery was followed up by an attack by the New Zealand Division in which 350 prisoners and 44 guns were taken. The New Zealanders then manoeuvred to try to cut off the retreat of the Ariete, but found themselves engaged by the Brescia Division of Italian X Corps in the depression of El Mreir. The third day of the battle closed with little further progress by either side having been made, but it was the British who could most feel pleased with themselves. The Axis advance to the Nile Delta had been stopped in the north, in the centre and in the south on the scratch defence line of El Alamein.

A battery of 88mm flak guns being used in an anti-tank role. The very high silhouette of the gun made it vulnerable to high-explosive counter-battery fire. (Bundesarchiv 1011-443-1574-24)

Rommel now realized that he and his troops had reached their limit; they were all exhausted. He had to accept that his quick dash for Cairo was over. He gave orders for the Afrika Korps to pull back from the line the next day and hand over their positions to Italian infantry. The field marshal had not given up on his goal of seizing the Suez Canal, he was just taking stock before he launched a renewed attempt. In the meantime, he ordered minefields to be laid and defensive positions to be dug. Auchinleck at the same time was trying to figure out his next move. He had stopped Rommel's attack and now outlined his future intentions to his corps commanders, Norrie and Gott. The Axis forces must be completely destroyed, he explained, and he would do this by containing the enemy's eastern and southern flanks then attacking his rear. The whole of XIII Corps, together with 7th Motor and 4th Armoured Brigades would drive into Rommel's right rear and then roll up Panzerarmee Afrika from the south. 'The enemy must be given no rest,' he ordered.

On 4 July the British moves began, but found that the German withdrawals they detected the night before had not taken place. Immediately the armoured brigades advanced they met an enemy anti-tank screen and were stopped. A little to the south the New Zealand Division applied pressure against an ineffectual Italian opposition at El Mreir and 1st Armoured Division probed gingerly in the north. All of these moves were half-hearted attempts, although they did clear the enemy off a great part of the Ruweisat Ridge. As the official history of the campaign commented: 'The 4th July was a day of disjointed engagements which had no significant results.' The troops of Eighth Army and their commanders were all tired; no great effort was forthcoming.

The next day Auchinleck tried to reposition his forces to continue with the left hook that he had planned, but eventually realized that with his limited amount of armour it might be more prudent to try a more shallow hook aimed at Deir el Shein. Both corps were now ordered to concentrate their efforts towards this depression to the south west of the

Ruweisat Ridge. This they did over the next few days, but again the results were disappointing, with little new ground taken. At the same time, Rommel reasoned that as Auchinleck was shifting more and more of his strength in the north, he might try a move in the south aimed at first taking Bab el Qattara, then sweeping northwards to get behind British XIII Corps. The attack was planned for 9 July.

Auchinleck was pre-warned of these moves by ULTRA intercepts and decided that he would also attack, this time in the far north from out of the Alamein Box. He ordered LtGen W.H. Ramsden, the new commander of XXX Corps, to capture Tel el Eisa and Tel el Makh Khad. Both were defended by Italians and air reconnaissance showed that their defences were not highly developed. The capture of these two features would put a salient into Rommel's positions from which mobile forces could move towards the Miteirya Ridge and Deir el Shein.

The move would also threaten the enemy's supply line along the coastal road. Gott's XIII Corps was to prevent the enemy reinforcing the coastal sector during the attack. Ramsden had the use of both the South African Division and the newly arrived Australian 9th Division for the operation. The attack was planned for 10 July.

On 9 July Rommel attacked the now abandoned Bab el Qattara defensive position. A set-piece assault was put in by 21st Panzer and the Littorio Armoured Division. Not surprisingly the move was completely successful. Rommel thought that he had found a weak spot and ordered his troops to thrust southwards to Qaret el Himeimat, also calling the 90th Light Division forwards to push eastwards to find a way around the Eighth Army's southern flank. As they did so, in the early hours of 10 July, a threatening rumble of guns was heard from the north. Auchinleck's forces were also on the move.

Australian 9th Division and South African 1st Division, backed by armour, attacked out of the Alamein Box behind a very strong artillery barrage of an intensity not yet seen in the desert. The Italians were taken completely by surprise and lost virtually the whole of the Sabratha Division and a large part of the Trieste. By 1000hrs the South Africans were on Tel el Makd Khad and the Australians had cleared the coastal side of the railway and were attacking Tel el Eisa, overrunning the important German radio intercept unit that had given Rommel so much information on British movements over the previous year.

On hearing news of the British attack, Rommel left Bab el Qattara and sped north, collecting a battle group of 15th Panzer Division on the way. He feared disaster, later admitting that he thought the enemy was in hot pursuit westwards scattering the fleeing Italians and destroying his supplies. The German 164th Division was at that time in the process of arriving on the front and its 382nd Regiment was immediately sent to engage the Australians. This counterattack was held by LtGen Morshead's division and the next day it succeeded in capturing the whole of Tel el Eisa. Over the next four days Rommel's forces tried again and again to evict the Australians from this feature covering the western approach to Alamein, but the Commonwealth troops held on to their gains. Unfortunately the South Africans had withdrawn from Tel el Makh Khad through some misunderstanding of their orders. Rommel had prevented a catastrophe, but at the expense of using the troops he was gathering for his own renewed advance. He now admitted that British Eighth Army was in the hands of a new commander who was deploying his forces 'with considerable skill.' Rommel was finally being forced to dance to someone else's tune.

On 12 and 13 July the enemy continued to attack the Tel el Eisa salient. Rommel also tried to cut it off by attacking the Alamein Box, but both efforts failed. On the night of 14 July Auchinleck launched a new attack along the line of the Ruweisat Ridge aiming to break through the enemy's centre. XXX and XIII Corps assaulted the ridge together. On the right, Indian 5th Division (XXX Corps) attacked Point 64 on the centre of the feature, the New Zealand Division (XIII Corps) was on the left attacking Point 63 at the western end of the ridge and the 1st Armoured Division gave support along the line of the inter-corps boundary. The night attack was preceded by Albacore aircraft dropping flares and fighter-bombers strafing the enemy lines.

At first both divisions made good progress as they fought their way through the Italian Brescia and Pavia Divisions who were holding the ridge. The advance slowed down when they met extensive minefields and there was some loss of cohesion when the New Zealanders were attacked by tanks from 8th Panzer Regiment of 15th Panzer Division and lost 350 prisoners. Throughout the day the pressure applied by the British forced the two Italian divisions to give way and by late afternoon of 15 July both Points 63 and 64 were taken and most of the ridge was in Eighth Army's hands. The 1st Armoured Division remained further back ready to exploit a breakthrough.

Rommel originally thought that the attack was just a large raid against the Ruweisat Ridge, believing that Auchinleck would continue with his main effort nearer the coast, but when news of the collapse of the Pavia and Brescia Divisions reached him he realized that something much bigger was afoot. He immediately ordered German troops to the spot. To lead the counterattack against Ruweisat Ridge Rommel used the reconnaissance units of his panzer divisions and these hit the New Zealanders with some force, pushing them off the western end of the feature. The ferocity of the attack carried the Panzer reconnaissance troops down the slopes, overrunning the HQ of 4th New Zealand

Brigade and capturing the whole of the HQ staff, including Brigadier Burrows. The British armour meanwhile continued to stand back and wait for the right moment to counter attack. The right moment never came, for the New Zealanders continued to be pushed back and the German advance only came to a halt when it brushed up against 1st Armoured Division itself. The day had been saved once again for the Axis army by Rommel's speedy deployment of scratch units and once again the field marshal had been given a nasty scare.

Auchinleck's attack had gained half of the Ruweisat Ridge, but had fallen well short of his original intentions. The early successes of the Indian and the New Zealand Divisions had not been exploited by the tanks and there remained a great antipathy between the armour and the infantry commanders. The Commonwealth troops in particular had a very poor opinion of the effectiveness of British tank support. Infantry/armour co-operation was at an all-time low.

During the night of 15 July Rommel remained concerned that the British would attack again with armour. To forestall this, the next day he ordered an assault to be made on the Indian 5th Division near Point 64. In the event this came to nothing. The Australians also attacked out of their salient at Tel el Eisa towards the Miteirya Ridge, but they, too, made little progress. The next day it was more of the same, both sides made attempts to take new ground only to be turned back by solid defences. One item of significance did take place, however, when the Desert Air Force managed to fly 641 sorties, a record number for a single day. At the end of Auchinleck's attacks all that had substantially changed was that the British held the eastern half of Ruweisat and were faced by Germans instead of Italians. None the less, much had still been achieved in that Rommel now abandoned any thought of further attacks. His situation had been made worse by the loss of 2,200 tons of ammunition and 50,000 gallons of fuel to the bombs of the Desert Air Force during raids on Matruh.

On 18 July, 7th Armoured Division sent light tanks and armoured cars out into the desert in the extreme south of the line to harass and confuse the flank of Panzerarmee Afrika.

These moves acted as a diversion, for Auchinleck was on the offensive again, trying to engineer the breakthrough that he still thought was within his grasp. Spurred on by the endless urgings of Churchill, Eighth Army's commander launched another assault. On 22 July, 5th Indian Division attacked along Ruweisat Ridge towards Deir El Shein and the New Zealand Division attacked the western end of the ridge and El Mreir Depression. Opposing them were the Italian Brescia Division in Deir el Shein and the 21st Panzer Division on the western end of the ridge. Both Commonwealth Divisions made it to their objectives, but both were evicted by the 5th and 8th Panzer Regiments before British armoured support could get up to them. When the British tanks did eventually make contact with the Germans they suffered tremendous casualties, losing 132 of their number during the day against the loss of just three of the enemy. Indian 5th Division tried again along the ridge on 23 July, but its efforts ended in failure.

Despite every attack failing to crack the enemy's defences, Auchinleck had still not given up on his desire of breaking through Rommel's line. Once again he switched his effort to the coastal sector and on 26 July, Australian 9th Division and South African 1st Division made an attempt to gain the eastern end of the Miteirya Ridge. Gaps were made in Axis minefields and infantry went through, but all efforts were repulsed before armoured support could get forward to help. The fighting spilled into the next day but the moment was lost and the abortive attack was called off.

Auchinleck now followed Rommel's earlier decision and also went on to the defensive. He issued instruction to his corps commanders to strengthen their defences, rehearse plans for meeting any enemy attack and to rest, reorganize and re-train their troops. Auchinleck was sure that Rommel would not resume his attacks before he had likewise rested and gained strength. The first battle of Alamein was over. Rommel had been stopped and the initiative had been wrested from him. Eighth Army was beginning to believe that Rommel could eventually be beaten, but there was still a long way to go and a lot of hard fighting to be done.

BATTLE OF ALAM HALFA

German Panzergrenadier lifting a British anti-tank mine prior to the Alam Halfa battle.
(IWM MH 5863)

uchinleck had stopped Panerarmee Afrika, but the danger had not gone away. Rommel's forces were still gathered within Egypt and were gaining strength for a new push into the Delta. In the north, Gen Navarini's Italian XXI Corps held the line, with German 164th Division superimposed on the Trento and Bologna Divisions between the sea and Deir el Shein. The southern sector was the responsibility of Italian X Corps, commanded by Gen Orsi, with the Brescia Division and GenMaj Ramcke's 288th Parachute Brigade holding from Deir el Shein to Gebel Kalakh. The Folgore Parachute Division guarded the remainder of the line southwards to Naqb abu Dweis. In reserve were the two mobile corps, with de Stefanis' XX corps containing the Ariete and Littorio Armoured Divisions and the Trieste Motorized Division, lined up in positions behind the infantry. Nehring's Afrika Korps with the 15th and 21st Panzer Divisions was in army reserve. The 90th Light Division was out of the line resting.

Facing the enemy, Eighth Army began to lay extensive minefields and organize defensive positions ready to receive Rommel's forces should they decide to continue the attack. The northern sector near the coast was held by Australian 9th Division of XXX Corps. Then came South African 1st Division and Indian 5th Division holding the line down to the Ruweisat Ridge. In reserve behind them was 23rd Armoured Brigade. South of the ridge was XIII Corps. The New Zealand 2nd Division and 7th Armoured Division held the line southwards to Himeimat. The 1st Armoured Division was the mobile reserve.

First Alamein was initially seen as a great victory, but this feeling soon turned into the depressing realization that Eight Army had achieved little in the long term. After over two years of fighting, the British were back where they started from. This state of affairs drew great criticism from those responsible for the direction of the war in London. Auchinleck further annoyed Churchill when he declared that he could not resume the attack against Rommel until at least the middle of September. He army was tired and needed reinforcement, resupply and retraining. Churchill, ever the belligerent, was beginning to lose patience. He conferred with his Cabinet and with his Chief of the Imperial General Staff, Gen Sir Alan Brooke, and decided that changes would be made.

There was much political manoeuvring about how these changes would be resolved, with Churchill and Brooke arguing as to who would be best for each job. A compromise was reached in August when they both visited Egypt, whereby Auchinleck was relieved of his command and replaced by Gen Sir Harold Alexander as C-in-C Middle East and LtGen Sir Bernard Montgomery was designated Commander Eighth Army. Montgomery was not Churchill's first choice, although he was

Brooke's. Churchill had originally insisted that there should be some continuity of command in the desert rather than a wholesale replacement of leaders from outside the theatre. He demanded that LtGen Gott should move from XXX Corps to take over Eighth Army, even though the corps commander was exhausted by his long stay in the desert and needed a rest. Churchill, as usual, got his own way and Gott was appointed to the command. Fate, however, intervened when Gott was killed a few days later in an air crash.

The appointment of Montgomery to the command of Eighth Army has been seen as one of the greatest strokes of good fortune of the war for the British Army. Virtually unknown outside the military when he arrived, Montgomery soon became Britain's greatest commander of the war. Great in terms of his successes and fame, but perhaps not so great in his pursuit of self-aggrandizement and in his relationships with others. For every admirer to which he could do no wrong, there was a detractor full of criticism regarding his conduct. But there is no doubt that his arrival in Eighth Army was a breath of fresh air. From the very moment he arrived he began moulding his new army into a formation that met with his rigid approval. After a two-year seesaw of victories and defeats, Montgomery was determined to 'kick Rommel out of Africa for good'.

LtGen Montgomery instigated many changes in his command. He urged much closer co-operation between ground forces and the Desert Air Force. He insisted that his divisions would fight as divisions together with all their supporting arms, there would be no more fragmentation of effort. He was adamant that he would not attack until his numerical strength was much greater than the enemy, and that all of his men were properly trained and equipped for the tasks they would be given in battle. He maintained that all of his orders would be meticulously carried out and that there would be no 'bellyaching'. At Alamein, as in all of his future battles, he would not move until he was ready and only then with overwhelming force. There was a new commander at the head of Eighth Army, and everyone knew it.

To command XIII Corps in place of Gott, Montgomery brought out LtGen Brian Horrocks from England. The forty-six-year-old Horrocks had worked with Monty in South Eastern Command and had impressed his boss with his energetic enthusiasm. He had seen action as a battalion commander in France in 1940 before taking over a brigade and then helped train both 44th and 9th Armoured Divisions as their GOC.

July and August were spent by both sides building up their forces ready to launch an attack. Just prior to the renewal of the advance eastwards the main tank strength of Panzerarmee Afrika was 443, comprising 200 German and 243 Italian tanks. Of these, twenty-six were the new Panzer IV Specials with the long 75mm gun, ten were older Panzer IVs with the short-barrel gun, 71 were Panzer IIIJs with the long 50mm gun and 93 Panzer IIIs with the old gun. All of the Italian tanks were various marks of the Medium M13/40. In addition the Germans had 29 light tanks and the Italians 38.

Rommel knew that time was most definitely not on his side. Reconnaissance showed that the British were laying extensive minefields and thickening their defences, especially in the northern sector near the coast and in front of the Ruweisat Ridge. The British with their short supply lines were also winning the battle of the build-up and were growing

German Panzergrenadier counts down the seconds to the start of an attack. (IWM HU5624)

stronger by the day. The strengthening of the British defences ruled out any hope of making an easy breakthrough in the north, or across the Ruweisat Ridge. The south seemed to be the area most favourable for his attack. This sector of the line was not as heavily fortified, although Eighth Army troops were still busy constructing new defences and extending their minefields even as Rommel watched.

German intelligence had also identified that a large convoy bringing over 100,000 tons of weapons, tanks, equipment and stores was due to arrive at Suez in early September. Rommel, on the other hand, with his extended lines and difficulties in transporting material across the Mediterranean, was finding it hard to assemble an effective force. He had to attack soon or face an even stronger enemy. He therefore decided to launch a new attempt to reach the Delta around the period of the full moon which was due on 26 August.

The German field marshal decided to employ the tried and tested tactics he had used previously in the assault, opting for a night attack through the British southern flank and an advance 45 kilometres eastwards past Alam Halfa ridge so that by dawn he could unleash his Afrika Korps northwards round the rear of Eighth Army's positions. The right flank of his attack would be protected by all of the highly mobile German and Italian reconnaissance units. Guarding the left flank would be the Ariete and Littorio Armoured Divisions of Italian XX Corps, with the rested 90th Light Division moving on the extreme northern flank of the assault. Rommel had great confidence in his troops and most especially in the Afrika Korps. This plan seemed to be the most promising, but to ensure success it relied on surprise, speed and having sufficient supplies available to support a mobile attack. To gain surprise Rommel planned to assemble his armoured forces by night and camouflage them by day. To mask the direction of the attack, diversionary raids and smaller attacks would be made in the north by Italian infantry.

It was a good plan, but one that was obvious to the British. Auchinleck had already concluded that the enemy assault would most probably be in the south, with an armoured thrust driving eastwards then swinging up behind Alam Halfa, and had taken steps to counter it. ULTRA intercepts had also confirmed that this was Rommel's intention, so when Montgomery arrived in Egypt to take command of the situation he was presented with advance warning of his opponent's overall strategy. This removed Rommel's element of surprise.

The key to the battle would be the Alam Halfa Ridge. If the Germans could get past it to the east, they could shift northwards and meet the British armour on favourable ground, behind the bulk of Eighth Army's positions. If Montgomery's forces could hold the ridge, then Rommel would not dare move further eastwards towards the Suez Canal with the whole of Eighth Army dominating his lines of communications. Montgomery therefore strengthened his forces on and around the feature. He brought forward the newly arrived 44th Division and lined up two of its brigades – 131st and 133rd Brigades – along the ridge with all of its divisional artillery and anti-tank guns. On the western end he placed 22nd Armoured Brigade from 10th Armoured Division. Further west the defensive position about Alam Nayil was held by the New Zealand Division, strengthened by the addition of 132nd Brigade. Just to the north, at the eastern end of Ruweisat Ridge, was XXX Corps' reserve, the

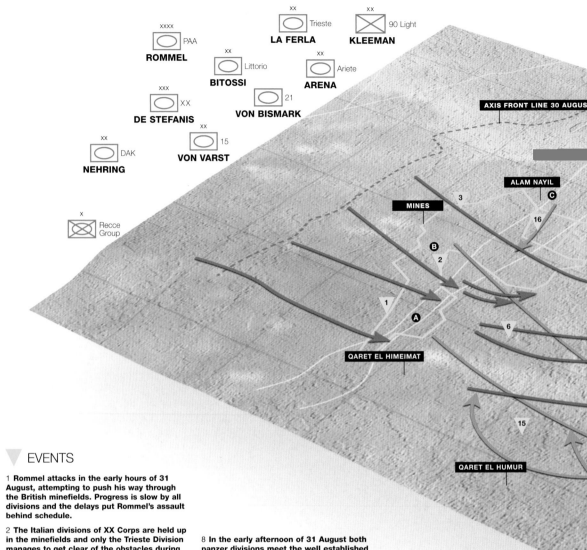

xx
Trieste
LA FERLA

xx
90 Light
KLEEMAN

xxxx
PAA
ROMMEL

xx
Littorio
BITOSSI

xx
Ariete
ARENA

xxx
XX
DE STEFANIS

21
VON BISMARK

xx
DAK
NEHRING

xx
15
VON VARST

AXIS FRONT LINE 30 AUGUST

ALAM NAYIL
C

3

16

MINES

B
2

1

A

6

QARET EL HIMEIMAT

15

QARET EL HUMUR

x
Recce
Group

EVENTS

1 **Rommel attacks in the early hours of 31 August, attempting to push his way through the British minefields. Progress is slow by all divisions and the delays put Rommel's assault behind schedule.**

2 **The Italian divisions of XX Corps are held up in the minefields and only the Trieste Division manages to get clear of the obstacles during the course of the battle.**

3 **The 90th Light Division also has difficulty crossing the British minefields and takes most of the first day trying to reach Deir el Muhafid.**

4 **After fighting a delaying action against the DAK, 4th Light Armoured Brigade falls back into 7th Armoured Division's positions around Samaket Gaballa**

5 **The 7th Motor Brigade delays Italian XX Corps and the 90th Light Division in the minefield then withdraws to Samaket Gaballa to join the rest of 7th Armoured Division.**

6 **The 15th and 21st Panzer Divisions finally get through the minefields later than expected and the delay forces Rommel to modify his original plan of passing to the east of Alam El Halfa. He now decides to turn his armoured divisions north before Alam El Halfa Ridge and strike towards the sea between that feature and the Ruweisat Ridge.**

7 **Once the direction of Rommel's attack becomes clear to Gen Montgomery, the Eighth Army's commander counters it by bringing his 23rd Armoured Brigade south alongside 22nd Armoured Brigade.**

8 **In the early afternoon of 31 August both panzer divisions meet the well established 22nd Armoured Brigade and fight an intense battle against British artillery and anti-tank guns. Unable to break through the defensive cordon, the attacks are broken off in the evening.**

9 **Early on 1 September the Panzer divisions try again to get past Alam el Halfa by moving to the east of 22nd Armoured Brigade. 15th Panzer Division is then struck by 8th Armoured Brigade which is moving across to join 22nd Armoured Brigade. Both formations are forced to a halt.**

10 **Montgomery further strengthens the Alam el Halfa position on 1 September by moving South African 2nd Brigade from XXX Corps to the north of the ridge.**

11 **Late on 1 September Rommel decides that he will have to call off the attack and go over to the defensive.**

12 **The next day, 2 September, Montgomery brings forward 151st Brigade from 50th Division to begin exerting pressure on the DAK.**

13 **In the south, 7th Armoured Division mounts probing attacks on the German Reconnaissance Group and the flanks of DAK.**

14 **On 2 September, Rommel orders a gradual withdrawal of all formations back to positions to the west of the British minefields.**

15 **The 7th Armoured Division continues its harassing attacks on the retreating Axis forces.**

16 **On the night of 3/4 September, New Zealand 2nd Division attacks southwards from its positions towards Deir el Muassib to harass the Axis withdrawal and to close the gaps in the minefields. The attack is met by stiff opposition and, after a day's fighting, is called off, allowing Rommel's forces to return to their original positions.**

ALAM EL HALFA: ROMMEL'S LAST CHANCE

This was Rommel's last attempt to break through to the Nile valley and he was anxious to gain a quick victory with dwindling resources. For Montgomery it was his introduction to the North Africa campaign and his first battle with the Eighth Army.

Note: Gridlines are shown at intervals of 5 miles

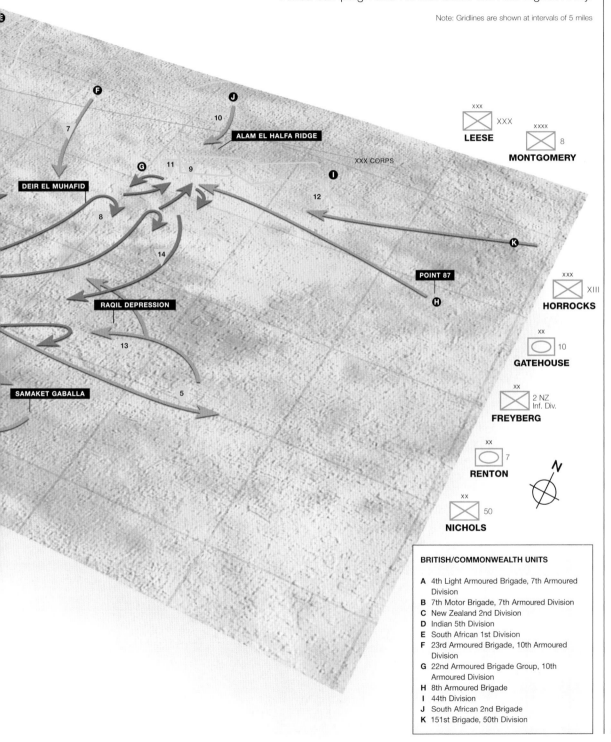

LEESE XXX

MONTGOMERY 8

XXX CORPS

HORROCKS XIII

GATEHOUSE 10

FREYBERG 2 NZ Inf. Div.

RENTON 7

NICHOLS 50

ALAM EL HALFA RIDGE

DEIR EL MUHAFID

RAQIL DEPRESSION

SAMAKET GABALLA

POINT 87

N

BRITISH/COMMONWEALTH UNITS

A 4th Light Armoured Brigade, 7th Armoured Division
B 7th Motor Brigade, 7th Armoured Division
C New Zealand 2nd Division
D Indian 5th Division
E South African 1st Division
F 23rd Armoured Brigade, 10th Armoured Division
G 22nd Armoured Brigade Group, 10th Armoured Division
H 8th Armoured Brigade
I 44th Division
J South African 2nd Brigade
K 151st Brigade, 50th Division

23rd Armoured Brigade. Monty planned to wait and see which way Rommel moved before committing the 23rd Armoured Brigade against him. Further to the east, around Point 87, was 10th Armoured Division's 8th Armoured Brigade. Holding the line in the south was 7th Armoured Division, with 4th Light Armoured Brigade and 7th Motor Brigade. Montgomery planned for these two brigades to try to hold any enemy attack, but to withdraw in the face of the German advance into positions around Samaket Gaballa. It was important that the division was kept intact and not overwhelmed by superior forces, for once the Afrika Korps had moved east, the 7th Armoured Division was to harry its flanks. To the north, XXX Corps was to hold the line with the three Dominion divisions already in place and absorb any diversionary attacks.

The element of speed required for Rommel's success was down to the Afrika Korps. It had to move its tanks through the British minefields and into open desert before dawn. Rommel was confident that it would. The third element essential for success, good supplies, and more importantly large quantities of petrol, was beyond Rommel's control. He had been promised adequate fuel for the attack, but the full moon of the 26 August came and began to wane while his fuel bunkers contained just the standard two days' worth of fuel. Nothing extra had reached Egypt or indeed North Africa. The supply situation for Panzerarmee Afrika was somewhat eased when Kesselring authorized the transfer of 1,500 tons of fuel from the Luftwaffe, enough for four days' usage. Further relief was promised by Cavallero, who insisted that a number of petrol tankers were due to arrive in Benghazi and Tripoli on 30 August. On these slim promises, Rommel steeled himself for battle and ordered the assault to go ahead as planned.

Rommel's attack got off to a poor start during the night of 30–31 August. Shortly after passing the eastern boundary of the Axis minefields

the attacking troops came up against unsuspected belts of British mines of such depth that the advance slowed almost to a halt. Intense artillery fire descended on Rommel's engineers and infantry as they tried to deal with an estimated 150,000 mines and booby traps which littered the sector of the attack. Whilst its men were engaged in the operation, the Afrika Korps was hit by relays of heavy bombers disrupting progress through the belt of obstacles. The two brigades of 7th Armoured Division fought well in defence and staged a controlled withdrawal as planned. The result was that none of the attacking formations had reached their appointed objectives by dawn. This delay in the timetable of the advance had ensured that the British were able to plot the route of the attack and be well prepared to receive the expected armoured thrust.

As news began to filter into Rommel's HQ the picture looked bleak. He acknowledged that the British had defended with extraordinary stubbornness and achieved a setback in his plan. He had hoped that by dawn his tanks would be 45 kilometres east of the minefields, ready to swing north towards the sea. Further bad news reached the army commander when he learned that GenMaj von Bismarck, commander of 21st Panzer Division had been killed by a mine and that Gen der Pz Nehring had been wounded in an air attack on his Afrika Korps. Rommel now considered abandoning the offensive, but decided to press on when he heard from Oberst Bayerlein, Nehring's Chief of Staff who had taken over command of the Afrika Korps, that the tanks were through the mines and driving east.

The delays suffered in the minefields and by air raids caused Rommel to reconsider his original plan. With the British alerted and ready, a wide sweep to the east, passing to the south of Alam Halfa Ridge, would expose his right flanks to the 7th Armoured Division and the 10th Armoured Division which he knew was in the north. He now decided to turn left before he got to Alam Halfa, much earlier than previously intended. New objectives were set: Point 132 on the ridge for the Afrika Korps and Point 102 at Alam Bueit for XX Corps. Then his forces would drive northwards passing behind the Ruweisat Ridge towards the coast road. But first the

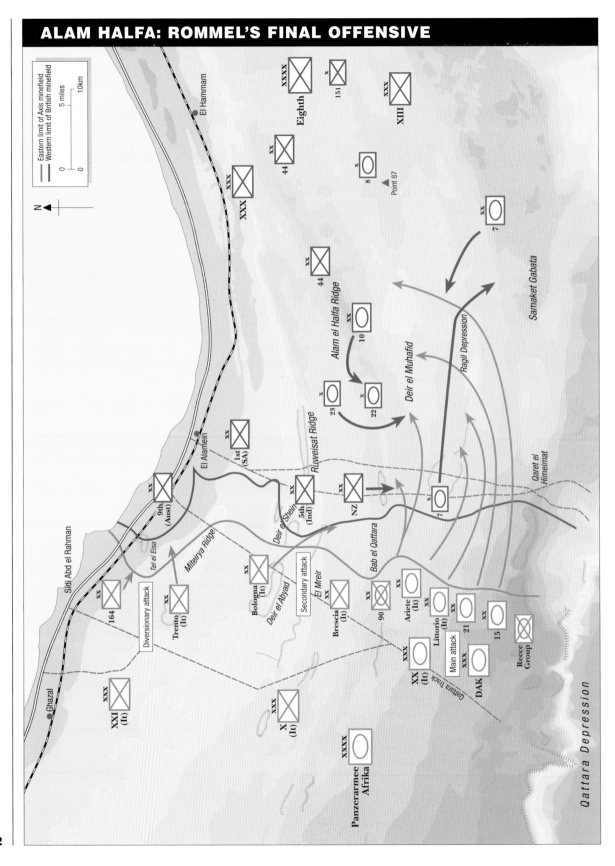

Eastern limit of Axis minefield
Western limit of British minefield

0 ——— 5 miles
0 ——— 10km

N

Eighth
151
XIII
44
44
8
Point 87
7
Alam el Halfa Ridge
10
Deir el Muhafid
Samaket Gabata
23
22
Ragil Depression
Ruweisat Ridge
1st (SA)
El Alamein
5th (Ind)
NZ
7
Qaret el Himeimat
Deir el Shein
Bab el Qattara
Sidi Abd el Rahman
El Hammam
Ghazal
Tel el Eisa
Miteirya Ridge
9th (Aust)
Diversionary attack
164
Trento (It)
Deir el Abyad
Bologna (It)
Secondary attack
El Mreir
Brescia (It)
90
Ariete (It)
Littorio (It)
21
15
Recce Group
XXI (It)
X (It)
Panzerarmee Afrika
XX (It)
Main attack
DAK
Qattara Track

Qattara Depression

A dead crewman lies beside his knocked-out Panzer III tank. (IWM E16494)

advance had to halt to refuel and take on ammunition. It was 1300hrs before it got going again.

Montgomery was pleased with the way things were shaping; the attack had come in just where it had been anticipated. The minefields were slowing down the advance as planned and throwing many of the Axis units into disarray. None of Italian XX Corps' divisions had managed to break free of the obstacles and 90th Light Division was virtually halted around Deir el Munassib. Best of all, the Afrika Korps was identified south of Alam Halfa and its direction of advance was aimed at the western end of the ridge itself. Montgomery could now confidently bring 23rd Armoured Brigade southwards to a position between 22nd Armoured Brigade and the New Zealanders. Rommel was being lured onto the hull-down tanks and anti-tank guns that were blocking his path.

The battle now took the course that Montgomery had hoped for. Both 15th and 21st Panzer Divisions ran into the defensive positions of the two British Armoured Brigades under the guns of division and corps artillery. Tank and anti-tank fire raked the advancing Germans and did great damage. Try as they might, the British armour could not be enticed out of their hull-down positions. It was now the Germans' turn to suffer the consequences of trying to overwhelm well established anti-tank guns and armour. When the light began to fade the attack was called off. The panzers withdrew to replenish their strength from dwindling stocks of fuel and ammunition.

Throughout the night, just as they had done during the long day, the Desert Air Force bombed and strafed the enemy. Flares lit up the night sky and the bright light etched out soft-topped transport, armour and guns on the bare desert below, exposing them to medium bombers and low flying fighter-bombers. None of the Axis troops were allowed any rest, for

The aftermath of the Alam Halfa action. British troops inspect the wrecked transport left on the battlefield by the Afrika Korps. (IWM E16651)

no sooner had one raid finished when another started. They lay all night in the sand, suffering the strain of waiting for the next bomb to fall.

Early the next day 15th Panzer Division tried to work around the eastern flank of 22nd Armoured Brigade. The move was frustrated by 8th Armoured Brigade moving across from Point 87 to join up with 22nd Armoured Brigade. Both sides were forced to a halt by supporting anti-tank fire. That day 21st Panzer Division did very little, frustrated by lack of fuel and strafed by artillery fire from the ridge. On the left flank of the Afrika Korps the Ariete and Littorio Divisions were still struggling to get clear of the minefields under continuous fire from the New Zealand Division. The Trieste Division did a little better, but still could not free itself from the artillery fire. Further north the 90th Light Division crawled forward past Munassib, never likely to get into the battle proper. By the end of the day, Rommel issued the order to his formations to go over to the defensive, dig themselves in and prepare for the next night of bombing.

Ever cautious, Montgomery now moved more formations to the Alam Halfa area. Now that all of the enemy's main force was committed, he was determined that they would get no further. He told XXX Corps to thin out its line and moved the South African 2nd Brigade further south to a position just north of the ridge. He also shifted Indian 5th Brigade southwards and brought it under command of Freyberg's New Zealand

Division. Super cautious, he then gave orders for 151st Brigade of 50th Division to cease its work as airfield protection back in the Delta and to come forward to the eastern end of the Alam Halfa Ridge. Rommel was now well and truly boxed in, for in the south, 7th Armoured Division was beginning to make sorties against his exposed flanks.

This was now the time for Montgomery to strike back and drive across Rommel's lines of communication to engineer a resounding defeat. The reinforcement of the New Zealand Division with Indian 5th Brigade came with a warning to LtGen Freyberg to get ready to attack southwards from Alam Nayil towards Himeimat. In the north, on 1 September Australian 9th Division carried out an operation west of Tel el Eisa and attacked German 164th Division, capturing 140 prisoners. This long-prepared move was planned to bring alarm to the Axis camp and to stress the vulnerability of their forces, strung out as they were across the desert.

Overhead fighters and bombers continued to plague the Afrika Korps. Joining with the Desert Air Force were a few squadrons of Mitchell bombers from the USAAF. They made 111 sorties on 1 September to join with the 372 flown by the RAF. That night they were active again over the Afrika Korps and included a few 4,000lb bombs in their loads with devastating effect.

Rommel knew that his offensive had failed. He had been held by a superior force arrayed on ground of its own choosing. He had also been let down by his superiors. Marshal Cavellero's promise of 5,000 tons of petrol failed to materialize: 2,600 tons of it had been sunk in the Mediterranean and 1,500 tons were still on the dockside in Italy. Just 900 tons were landed and much of that was consumed by transport on its long journey to the front. Kesselring's assurance of 1,500 tons of Luftwaffe fuel to be delivered by air was also a hollow gesture. Only a fraction of it arrived. On 2 September, Rommel ordered a gradual withdrawal of all formations back to the western edge of the British minefields.

Rommel was puzzled by Montgomery's tactics. He knew that the British had assembled a powerful armoured force between Alam Halfa and Bab el Qattara, but it had remained stationary in its assembly area. The impression he gained of the new British commander was 'of a very cautious man who was not prepared to take any sort of risk.' Montgomery was indeed acting cautiously. He judged Eighth Army to be unready to take on the task of a possible chase and ordered that the enemy was to be harassed vigorously, but the only staged attack was the one to be launched by LtGen Freyberg's division. This itself was to be limited to the closing of the minefield gaps behind the Axis forces and was not due to take place before the night of 3/4 September, almost two days after Rommel had begun his withdrawal.

Monty's counterattack finally began with diversionary raids by 6th New Zealand Division at 2300hrs on 3 September. These roused the enemy who met the advancing infantry of 132nd Brigade with mortar and machine-gun fire disrupting its advance, although a similar attack by New Zealand 5th Brigade did reach its initial objectives. Strong fighting went on throughout the night as the Italians and Germans fought to prevent the gaps being closed. Progress was poor and shortly after midday on 4 September the enemy came back at the New Zealand Division in a fierce counterattack. This was successfully turned aside,

TANKS AND MOTORIZED INFANTRY FROM 15TH PANZER DIVISION ATTACK TOWARDS ALAM HALFA RIDGE ON 1 SEPTEMBER (pages 56–57)

GFM Rommel's last attempt to break through Eighth Army's lines at El Alamein and drive on towards the Nile Delta was delayed by the strength and depth of British minefields. When his Afrika Korps finally emerged from the eastern limit of the obstacles and manoeuvred to get behind the main British positions, Rommel was forced to try to swing his armour around the western end of the Alam Halfa Ridge to make up for lost time. Montgomery tracked this movement and brought 23rd Armoured Brigade southwards to a position between 22nd Armoured Brigade and the New Zealanders to block the move. Rommel's panzers had been lured onto a mass of hull-down tanks and anti-tank guns blocking his path. The battle then took the course that Montgomery had hoped for. Both 15th and 21st Panzer Divisions had to face the defensive positions of the two British brigades and the 44th Division. They were caught by a welter of fire from division and corps artillery, which raked the advancing Afrika Korps with tank and anti-tank shells. Panzers and Panzergrenadiers suffered considerably trying to overwhelm these well-established guns without being able to entice the British armour out of their hull-down positions. The Battlescene shows tanks of the 15th Panzer Division attacking towards Alam Halfa

Ridge on 31 August through the barrage of British fire. At this stage of the campaign, 15th Panzer Division had perfected its mobility and always attacked with infantry support. The troops of the motorized 115th Panzergrenadier Regiment were carried forward in SdKfz 251 half-track armoured personnel carriers (1) and trucks, which allowed them to immediately exploit any gains made by the armour. Amongst the division were a few of the improved Panzer IV tanks (2) with the long 75mm gun known to the British as a 'MarkIV Special'. This up-gunned tank was master of the battlefield, outperforming all other tanks. Unfortunately for Rommel, only a few of them were available to the Afrika Korps for Alam Halfa and the bulk of his armour consisted of older Panzer IIIs and short-barrelled Panzer IVs. When the new Panzer IVs finally did appear in North Africa in significant numbers, the Allies had by then also received a new tank with comparable performance in the shape of the Sherman. The 15th Panzer Division was formed from the 33rd Infantry Division which had taken part in the campaign in France in 1940. It arrived in North Africa in 1941 with one panzer regiment (the 8th) and two Panzergrenadier regiments (the 104th and the 115th) and became the founding division of the Afrika Korps. A short time later it gave up its 104th Panzergrenadier Regiment to join with 5th Panzer Regiment to the form the new 21st Panzer Division. (Howard Gerrard)

then a second attack took place a few hours later. Artillery fire backed up by day bombers helped to break up both assaults. The enemy's fierce reaction convinced Freyberg that a renewed attack by his division would not succeed and he requested permission for a complete withdrawal. This was granted by both Horrocks and Montgomery.

The attempt to close the minefields and to show at least some sign of aggressive action had failed. Even the British official history admits that 'it had caused the enemy no more than passing concern.' It did, however, give the New Zealand Division itself some cause for concern, for it lost 275 men, including the capture of its 6th Brigade's commander, Brig Clifton. The 132nd Brigade fared even worse, with 697 killed, wounded and missing, among whom was its commander, Brig Robertson. It was a very disappointing outcome for such a high number of casualties. Total British casualties after almost a week of fighting amounted to 1,750 killed, wounded and missing. The Italians lost 1,051 men and the Germans 1,859. The Germans had 38 tanks destroyed and the Italians 11, while the British lost 67. In the air, losses in aircraft from all causes were British 68, Italian 5 and German 36.

The Battle of Alam Halfa ended with Panzerarmee Afrika withdrawing all of its formations to the western side of the British minefields unmolested, except for some light actions fought by the 7th and 10th Armoured Divisions following at a safe distance. Montgomery even left Axis forces in possession of the high ground at Himeimat, claiming that he rather liked them to overlook his southern front so that they could see the bogus preparations being made for his coming offensive and perhaps believe that his main attack would be launched in the south.

EL ALAMEIN: THE ATTACK

Gen Montgomery was quite satisfied with the outcome of the Alam Halfa battle. He felt that the application of his tactics had demonstrated that the revitalized Eighth Army under his command was more than capable of defeating Rommel. As soon as the battle was over, all of Montgomery's energy was concentrated on his proposed offensive to break Panzerarmee Afrika. Every man in Eighth Army, from its commander down to its rank and file, now applied himself to the preparations for the coming battle.

The first task was to replace and strengthen the minefields that were lost in the German breakthrough. Next, a programme of training rolled out through the army as each formation rehearsed the techniques that were required for the task that had been allocated to it in the attack. Much new equipment was arriving in Egypt and troops were required to adjust to the new demands placed upon them. Units were reshuffled to bring them under their appropriate command; Montgomery insisted that divisions must fight as divisions with all of the support units that were proper to them. There would be no brigade groups as had been common in the past, except in the case of the Greek and French contingents. They would still operate independently with their own support units.

One of the first things that Montgomery did when he arrived in Egypt was to create a mobile corps of armour which he termed his *corps de chasse.*

He envisaged that the formation would be the British equivalent of the Afrika Korps; an armoured strike force that could exploit any breakthrough made in the enemy lines. He chose X Corps for this task and moved LtGen Lumsden across from 1st Armoured Division to take over the reformed corps. Lumsden was not Monty's first choice for the command; he would have preferred to have someone he knew in charge of the corps, but pressure was applied by Alexander to employ one of the existing Eighth Army commanders who had both desert and armoured experience.

Montgomery brought into X Corps the 1st, 10th and the newly arrived 8th Armoured Divisions, together with the 2nd New Zealand Division which had been reorganized by the addition of British 9th Armoured Brigade. The 7th Armoured Division remained with Horrocks' XIII Corps.

Many changes now took place amongst the senior officers, for there was a great weeding

A British film cameraman takes a look inside a knocked out Italian M13/40 Italian tank. The turret is facing to the rear. (IWM E14556)

out of unsuitable, over-age and ineffective commanders. The biggest change was the removal of LtGen Ramsden as commander of XXX Corps. He was replaced by a newcomer from England, LtGen Oliver Leese, from Guards Armoured Division. MajGen Renton left 7th Armoured Division to be replaced by MajGen A.F. Harding who moved over from his post as Deputy Chief of Staff in Cairo. Lower down the chain of command, more new men with new ideas were promoted to replace those that Montgomery deemed to be out of touch or tired.

There was a great deal of pressure being applied to Alexander to persuade Montgomery to launch his attack sooner rather than later. Churchill was pushing for a resounding victory over Rommel before the proposed Anglo-American landings in Morocco and Algeria took place. These were planned for early November and it was important that the Vichy French in those countries, and in Tunisia, were influenced in the Allies' favour before the Americans arrived. An Axis defeat in North Africa would go some way in persuading the French colonials not to oppose the landings. It was also important that fresh convoys got through to the besieged island of Malta whose population was near to starvation. These convoys could not sail until the enemy had been cleared from airfields in nearby Cyrenaica. Churchill pressed for the attack to be made in late September, but Montgomery would not be swayed from his target launch date of mid-October. He was determined not to move until he was absolutely ready.

On 3 September the promised shipment of 300 American Sherman tanks arrived at Suez to be dispersed amongst the armoured brigades, usually one squadron per armoured regiment. The build-up of armour continued with British-built tanks also arriving in greater numbers. By the start of the offensive Eighth Army's effective tank strength ready for action was 1,038, comprising 252 Shermans, 170 Grants, 294 Crusaders, 119 Stuarts, 194 Valentines, six Matildas and three Churchills. In addition there were around 200 of all types available as replacements. Also arriving were large numbers of the new 6-pdr anti-tank gun and more of the smaller 2-pdr gun. At the start of the battle there were 554 2-pdr and 849 6-pdr anti-tank guns in operation. This meant that all of the Royal Artillery anti-tank regiments were now equipped with the effective 6-pdr guns, each more than capable of dealing with Axis armour. In support, the Royal Artillery had 52 medium guns and 832, 25-pdr field pieces. The fire power of Eighth Army had more than doubled during the critical weeks leading up to Montgomery's offensive. Supplies were plentiful, vast quantities of fuel and ammunition were available from stocks in the Delta and were being delivered along short lines of communication well served by road and rail. These improvements, coupled with the changes in command and the reorganization of units and formations, brought an air of renewed confidence and vigour amongst the 195,000 men who made up the fighting strength of Eighth Army.

It only remained for Montgomery to formulate a plan that would break Rommel's line and force Panzerarmee Afrika into retreat. With no room to manoeuvre a mobile striking force of armour around the enemy's flank, Montgomery was constrained to force a passage right through his main defensive zones. He therefore decided that his main attack would be made in the north by XXX Corps, with a subsidiary assault in the south by XIII Corps. Deception plans would be used to make the enemy believe that the southern attack was in fact the main effort, for it would be strong enough to prevent the enemy moving troops to reinforce the northern sector. Montgomery's original plan relied on the armour of Lumsden's X Corps helping to carve out a passage through the German defences, but reluctance which verged on mutiny by the armoured commanders swayed Monty into changing his intentions. He settled on a plan which would rely on simultaneous attacks by four infantry divisions to help clear routes through which the armoured divisions could advance. The armoured divisions would then themselves clear two corridors through the minefields passable for tanks. Then the infantry would widen their breaches to the north and south by methodically destroying enemy troops, 'crumbling' away the Axis defenders by overwhelming artillery fire and local attacks. Rommel could not stand idle and watch his defences disintegrate; he would have to commit his armour to help save his infantry. The British tank force would then manoeuvre through the breaches to meet the counterattack by the Panzer divisions.

A British sergeant looking out across the Qattara Depression. This vast area of soft sand was thought to be impenetrable to most vehicles and therefore anchored the southern end of the El Alamein defence line. (IWM E16399)

The overwhelming strength of the land forces that Montgomery was able to put in the field, was similarly matched by the British effort in the air. Air Vice-Marshal Coningham had 104 squadrons at his disposal from the RAF, Dominion and USAAF units. He could put 530 serviceable aircraft aloft against the 350 serviceable aircraft available to Axis air forces (150 German and 200 Italian). Coningham planned to attack the enemy's airfields by day and night and to provide fighter cover over the army's forward area. He would also provide constant reconnaissance over the enemy positions before the attack while at the same time interdicting any Axis attempts to spy on British preparations. Once the battle began, Coningham intended to provide constant ground support as required. There was to be complete army and air force co-operation. Even the Royal Navy was to participate in the action, planning disruptive demonstrations along the coast to simulate landings in the rear of Rommel's forces.

To the west of Eighth Army, ensconced behind thick minefields, Panzerarmee Afrika was not so full of confidence. Visions of capturing Cairo and the Suez Canal had faded from their memories. The Germans and Italians waited in their exposed dugouts sure in the knowledge that the big attack was coming. They had no illusions about what was in store for them. They knew that their once mobile army had been reduced to a static role, just waiting for the enemy to strike. Most of the Italians were now longing for the end of the war. Successful British attacks by sea and air against shipping had meant that supplies were short, ammunition was scarce and fuel was rationed. Replacements in manpower had not kept pace with losses, with the inevitable result that all formations were below strength. To make matters worse, their inspiring commander was gone, invalided home to Germany for a rest.

Rommel's health had deteriorated during the campaign. He had pushed himself hard for two years and had taken little rest; by the end of the Alam Halfa battle he was near to collapse. His doctor ordered him home for at least six weeks' leave to recuperate. Rommel was replaced by *Gen der Kavallerie* Georg Stumme who had commanded Rommel's old 7th Panzer Division and then XXXX Panzer Korps on the Russian Front.

Before he left, Rommel spent the first two weeks of September reorganizing his formations to meet the coming attack which he expected to take place early in October. He knew that the British had overwhelming superiority both on land and in the air but would not choose to fight a mobile battle against his Afrika Korps. He was therefore forced to base his defence on a static fortified line against which he knew the British would use their massed artillery. The battle would start with an infantry attack which would have to carve a way through the defences for their tanks to follow. As a result Rommel knew that his plan of defence was simple: the line must be made as strong as possible with the main positions capable of holding out against the heaviest assault long enough for the Panzer divisions to come to their aid. He also supposed that the initial assault would be made at several places, with Montgomery looking to exploit the most favourable penetration.

The Axis line was to be held by Italian troops interlaced with German units. Italian and German formations were superimposed on top of each other right down to battalion level to stiffen the Italian resolve and bring German expertise into the defence. Rommel kept his two main tank formations to the rear of the defences, with 15th Panzer Division in the northern sector and 21st Panzer Division in the south. De Stefanis' XX Corps was split up, with the Littorio Armoured Division in front of 15th Panzer and the Ariete in the south together with 21st Panzer. In reserve by the coast, but well to the west of the main line, were 90th Light Division and the Trieste Motorized Division. From the coast down to the Miteirya Ridge the main line was held by German 164th Division and Gen Gloria's Italian XXI Corps, with Trento Division overlapping the positions held by the 164th. From there to Deir el Shein and Ruweisat Ridge was covered

Italian signal men repairing a break in the communications line. All lines had to be laid across open ground and the passage of tanks and lorries over them caused breaks that needed almost constant attention. Most contact between formations in forward areas had to be by radio. (Ufficio Storico Esercito Rome)

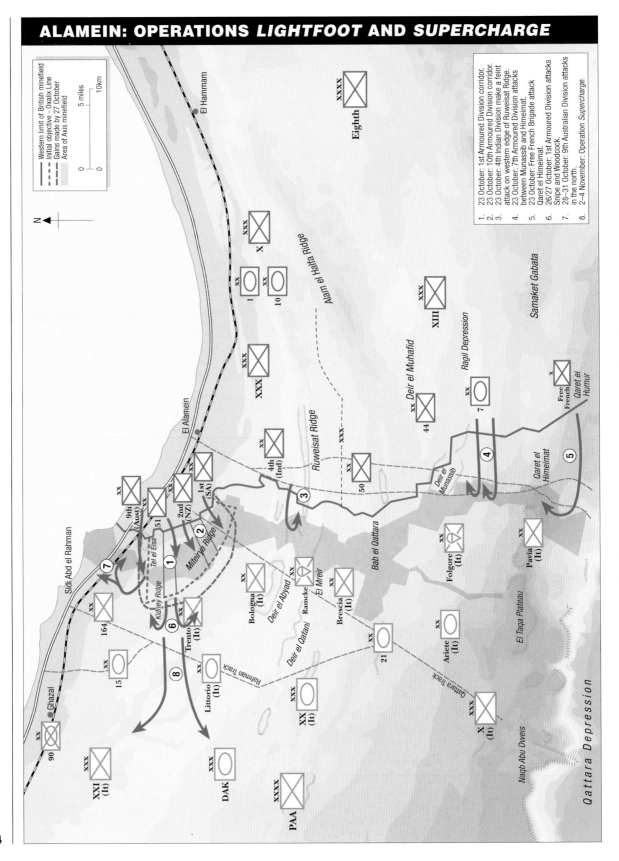

ALAMEIN: OPERATIONS *LIGHTFOOT* AND *SUPERCHARGE*

Western limit of British minefield
Initial objective - Oxalix Line
Gains made by 27 October
Area of Axis minefield

0   5 miles
0   10km

N

1. 23 October: 1st Armoured Division corridor.
2. 23 October: 10th Armoured Division corridor.
3. 23 October: 4th Indian Division make a feint attack on western edge of Ruweisat Ridge.
4. 23 October: 7th Armoured Division attacks between Munassib and Himeimat.
5. 23 October: Free French Brigade attack Qaret el Himeimat.
6. 26/27 October: 1st Armoured Division attacks Snipe and Woodcock.
7. 28–31 October: 9th Australian Division attacks in the north.
8. 2–4 November: Operation *Supercharge*.

Eighth

X

XX 1
XX 10

Alam el Halfa Ridge

XIII

XXX 44

Ragil Depression

Samaket Gabata

XXX
Free French

Deir el Muhafid

XX 7

Qaret el Himeimat

El Alamein

4th (Ind)

Ruweisat Ridge

XXX 50

Deir el Munassib

Bab el Qattara

El Taqa Plateau

1st (SA)

9th (Aust)
51
2nd (NZ)

Tel el Eisa
Miteirya Ridge
Kidney Ridge

Sidi Abd el Rahman

Ghazal

90

XXI (It)

DAK

PAA

164

15

Littorio (It)

Trento (It)

Bologna (It)

Deir el Abyad
Ramcke
El Mreir
Brescia (It)

Deir el Qatani

Rahman Track

21

Ariete (It)

Folgore (It)

Pavia (It)

Qattara Track

X (It)

Naqb Abu Dweis

Qattara Depression

by the Bologna Division. To the south of these positions was Gen Frattini's X Corps, with the Brescia Division around Bab el Qattara. Both the Bologna and the Brescia Divisions were 'sandwiched' with battalions of Ramcke's Parachute Brigade. The remainder of the line southwards to Qaret el Himeimat contained the Folgore Parachute Division and the Pavia Division.

The Axis defences were designed in depth, beginning with a thin screen of outposts on the edge of the forward minefields, with some section posts actually in the minefields themselves. The minefields were strewn with both anti-tank and anti-personnel mines, linked together with booby traps and other obstacles. A German report just before the battle suggested that there were 445,000 mines in the Axis minefields, about 14,000 of which were antipersonnel type. These advance positions would contain a company of infantry with a few anti-tank guns and machine guns. The lightly held zones located well forward enabled the main line of defence and the heavier anti-tank guns to be placed to the rear, further away from British artillery. About two kilometres behind these advance positions was the principal minefield belt with strong defensive locations along its front edge. Each Axis battalion would hold a sector of the line about one-and-a-half kilometres long and five kilometres deep. The main position would contain the bulk of the anti-tank and machine guns. The depth of the line from the forward positions to the rear of the defensive zone was between four and seven kilometres. Behind this were the heavy artillery and then the Panzer divisions, waiting to bring their fire onto any possible penetration. It was important for Rommel to confine the British within this defended zone. Rommel knew that if the British armour ever managed to break out into the open, then the battle would be virtually lost.

Rommel relied on his instinct that the British would attack in their usual manner, saturating the forward positions with devastating artillery fire and then putting in an infantry assault. This would give ample warning to the main defence line of the direction and strength of the attack. By the time the main line was reached, the initial surprise would have been lost and the impetus of the attack would be starting to wane. The advancing infantry would then be met with the strongest part of the defences. Any attempt to push armour through at this point would be countered by the anti-tank screen which in all probability would have been missed by the artillery bombardment. As the battle progressed, any likely penetration could then be countered by shifting into that sector the whole or part of one of the armoured divisions.

The effective tank strength of the Panzer divisions was well below their peak, with 249 German and 278 Italian main tanks and just 20 light tanks available for action. In anti-tank guns, the Axis forces contained 68 7.65cm guns, and 290 5cm Pak 38s. Of the potent dual-role 8.8cm flak guns, Rommel never had enough and never stopped asking for more. At the start of the battle 19th Flak Division deployed 86 of these weapons in the forward area and a further 52 in the rear areas for anti-aircraft defence of the airfields and ports. The fighting strength of Panzerarmee Afrika was around 104,000, of which 54,000 were Italian and 50,000 German.

While Montgomery had been switching many of his senior commanders because of a perceived lack of ability, Rommel was obliged to change some of his for more depressing reasons. The wounded Nehring was replaced by GenLt Wilhelm Ritter von Thoma as head of the Afrika

Korps. Von Thoma came from Russia with a growing reputation as an armoured commander. GenMaj Heinz von Randow replaced the dead von Bismarck at the head of 21st Panzer Division and GenLt Graf von Sponeck succeeded the wounded Kleeman in 90th Light Division. Such an influx of new senior commanders did little to improve confidence amongst Axis forces, but it was the loss of their lucky talisman, GFM Rommel, that hit them most.

Before Rommel left for his rest in Austria, he met with Marshal Cavellero and demanded that shipments of supplies to Panzerarmee Afrika be increased. He asked for at least 30,000 tons to be delivered in September and 35,000 tons in October. Cavellero reassured him that every effort would be made to meet these totals. On his way to Germany Rommel repeated his demands to Mussolini and then again to Hitler and Göring when he arrived in Berlin a few days later, but was left with a feeling that little would be done.

The battle was set to begin on the night of 23 October. Lined up that night along the edge of the British minefields were XXX and XIII Corps. LtGen Leese's XXX Corps was on the right with, from north to south, 9th Australian Division, 51st (Highland) Division, 2nd New Zealand Division, 1st South African Division and 4th Indian Division. These were in the line from the coast to the south of the Ruweisat Ridge. From there to the Qattara Depression was Horrocks' XIII Corps containing 50th Division, 44th Division, 7th Armoured Division and 1st French Brigade. Lumsden's X Corps, with 1st and 10th Armoured Divisions, was in the rear of XXX Corps near the coast. The recently arrived 8th Armoured Division was destined not to take part in the battle as a division. It had been split, with its 24th Armoured Brigade under the command of 10th Armoured Division and the remainder of the division grouped together into a formation called 'Hammerforce' and placed under the command of 1st Armoured Division.

Montgomery's final orders for the offensive, code named 'Lightfoot', called for three simultaneous attacks to be made. In the north, XXX Corps would penetrate the enemy line and form a bridgehead beyond the main Axis defence zone, advancing to a forward position code named 'Oxalic', then assist X Corps to pass through. In the south, XIII Corps would penetrate the enemy positions near Munassib and pass the 7th Armoured Division through towards Jebel Kalakh. The division was told

Italian Semovente 75/18 self-propelled gun. This vehicle consisted of a turretless medium M40 tank chassis mounted with a 75mm gun, which made it a very potent, but unreliable, weapon. (Ufficio Storico Esercito Rome)

not to get itself into a slogging match, but to preserve its strength for later mobile operations, its main task to threaten the enemy in order to keep his armour in the south. Finally, XIII Corps would use the 1st French Brigade to secure the Qaret el Himeimat and the El Taqa plateau. Both XXX and XIII Corps were then to begin the crumbling operations to grind down the enemy infantry and draw the Panzers onto the armoured divisions and the massed anti-tank guns. If the enemy armoured divisions failed to come forward to meet the challenge, 1st and 10th Armoured Divisions were to seek positions from which they could prevent the enemy from interfering with XXX Corps' crumbling operations.

The main weight of Eighth Army's assault was with XXX Corps. Four of its divisions were to attack Axis minefields and defences then help carve out two cleared corridors for the armoured divisions. On the right, 9th Australian Division would attack eastwards from Tel El Eisa; on its left, 51st Division would clear a path towards Kidney Ridge. Both of these divisions would cover the ground of 1st Armoured Division's northern corridor through the enemy minefields. South of these divisions, 2nd New Zealand Division would clear towards the western end of the Miteiriya Ridge and 1st South African Division would attack across the main part of the ridge. These would then cover the southern corridor through the minefields for 10th Armoured Division. On the extreme left of XXX Corps, the 4th Indian Division would take no major part in the opening attack, but would make threatening and diversionary raids from the western end of Ruweisat Ridge.

The battle opened with a tremendous artillery barrage at 2140hrs on 23 October. At first the guns opened up on the known locations of all enemy gun sites with anti-battery fire. This fire then switched to the forward edge of the enemy defences. As the infantry attacked, the artillery laid down a rolling barrage in front of them, lifting by measured amounts as the infantry moved forward. For the first time in the desert, there were sufficient anti-tank guns protecting the infantry to allow all of the 25-pdr weapons to be massed together under centralized command in their proper role as field guns. Medium and heavy guns of the Royal Artillery were added to produce the greatest concentrated barrage since the First World War. Ammunition supplies were unrestricted allowing the

guns to fire at a prodigious rate. In the following twelve days of fighting, the 834 field guns fired altogether over one million rounds, an average of 102 rounds per gun per day. The rates for the other guns were even higher; 133 rounds for the 4.5in guns and 157 for the 5.5in weapons.

The Desert Air Force added its weight to the bombardment by bombing known enemy gun positions and those German and Italian guns which returned fire. Specially equipped Wellington bombers also flew overhead, jamming the radio-telephony channels of the Axis forces in an effort to disrupt enemy communications. These measures effectively blocked off radio traffic for a period, adding to the confusion at Panzerarmee's HQ as to the size and direction of the attack.

The four divisions of XXX Corps attacked together on a 16km front, each with two brigades forward. Each division had one regiment of Valentine tanks from 23rd Armoured Brigade in support, except Freyberg's New Zealanders who had the whole of 9th Armoured Brigade under command. The four formations advanced across a kilometre of no-man's-land and then began their attack through six kilometres of enemy-held territory towards their objective, phase line 'Oxalic'.

Nearest the sea, the Australians attacked with 26th Brigade on the right and the 20th Brigade on the left. Its third brigade, 24th Brigade, made noisy feints towards the coast in an effort to draw fire. The right brigade reached 'Oxalic' after some fierce encounters with the enemy, but 20th Brigade was stopped about a kilometre short by stiff resistance. The Australian Division endured the same pattern of events that was being experienced by other attacking divisions. The first minefield and line of defence was crossed with no great difficulty, just as Rommel expected them to be. But, as the two brigades pushed on into the main German defence line and the second minefield, enemy resistance increased.

On the left of the Australians, the Highlanders of 51st Division advanced on a two-brigade front with 153rd Brigade on the right and 154th Brigade on the left. Each brigade moved with one battalion forward and the other two ready to follow up. They set out to the stirring sounds of regimental pipers marching at the head of the battalions. In order to maintain the momentum, when each intermediate phase line was reached, the

Royal Engineer mine-clearance teams were amongst the most valuable troops on the battlefield. The numbers of mines laid in front of both opposing armies was prodigious and little forward progress could be made until they had been lifted to allow tanks and vehicles to pass through. (IWM E16226)

forward battalion paused while the battalion to its rear leapfrogged over into the lead. This procedure was repeated across other phase lines towards 'Oxalic'. The Highland Division had the most difficult task of XXX Corps, for its final objectives covered a width double the front of its start line. There was also a larger number of defended localities to be overcome, each of which had to be eliminated before the advance could continue. Progress at first was good, but it was gradually slowed down by the large numbers of casualties that the division was suffering. By dawn the Highland Division had not penetrated the enemy's main defence line. The delays and difficulties met during the advance meant that the mine clearance teams hoping to open a corridor for 1st Armoured Division were delayed.

The 2nd New Zealand Division began its attack on the western end of Miteirya Ridge also on a two-brigade front, with just one battalion at a time in the lead. LtGen Freyberg had decided to use his two infantry brigades to fight their way to the ridge before introducing the full strength of 9th Armoured Brigade to pass through and get beyond the high ground. He wanted to save as much of his weight as he could for this final stage. The plan worked well and the New Zealander infantry, despite heavy casualties, cleared a way through the minefields to allow Brig Currie to get his tanks on the crest of the ridge just before dawn. The coming of daylight, however, brought accurate enemy fire which forced the armour back on to the reverse slopes.

MajGen Pienaar's 1st South African Division advanced in much the same method as the New Zealanders. The infantry penetrated the minefields and cleared a way for some armoured support and the division was able, with great effort, to get onto the eastern end of the ridge. Difficulty was met in trying to get vehicles and heavy weapons forward which limited the strength of the division's positions. It had hoped to get beyond the ridge and allow armoured cars and the tanks of 8th RTR to exploit the left hand of XXX Corps attack, but enemy resistance forced it to dig in along the ridge. Just a little further south, Indian 4th Division made threatening raids near Ruweisat Ridge to confuse the enemy with regard to the length of the main British attack.

In the main, the first twelve hours of XXX Corps' attack had been fairly successful. LtGen Leese had got his divisions through most of the minefields and well into the enemy's positions. Best of all, he had troops on the Miteirya Ridge, something that Rommel would have been horrified by had he been on the spot. This success was not mirrored during the night by X Corps. Each of its armoured divisions had the responsibility of clearing its own minefield gaps. The clearance teams were to work closely with the infantry to open three gaps for its parent division, each wide enough for tanks. It was planned that these gaps would be completely swept and marked during the hours of darkness, allowing the armoured divisions to exploit southwards from XXX Corps final objectives before dawn. They would then be ready to meet the expected Panzer counterattacks on ground of their own choosing. Unfortunately, this did not happen.

The corps had priority on all forward tracks from 0200hrs. Its clearance teams came forward as planned but then worked in confusing and hazardous conditions to locate and clear mines by hand and with mine detectors. The northern corridor for 1st Armoured Division was located close to the junction of the Australian and Highland Divisions. Results that night were mixed with one marked gap actually completed through as far as the forward infantry, but the others slowed down by pockets of enemy resistance close to their routes. The other gap for 10th Armoured Division was located in the New Zealand sector further south. Here there was a little more success with four routes marked right up to the Miteirya Ridge, although only one was actually usable at the western end. Immense traffic jams at the eastern end of all the routes prevented many tanks getting through to the forward edge of the penetration. Those that did were met with heavy anti-tank fire from many parts of the enemy main defences that were still intact. By dawn his fire forced those tanks that had made it onto the ridge back over the crest to hull-down positions in the rear. In some cases the armour made a complete withdrawal right back off the ridge. When daylight came, neither 1st nor 10th Armoured Divisions were in a position to exploit XXX Corps' penetration.

Down in the south, Horrocks' XIII Corps had put in its attack the previous night in concert with those in the north. MajGen Harding's 7th Armoured Division met the same resistance and difficulties when trying to penetrate the minefields as had the divisions of XXX and X Corps. The division's right flank was protected by an attack by 131st Brigade of 44th Division which ran into difficulties soon after the start. Only the first of two large enemy minefields was actually penetrated by XIII Corps before dawn, but the attack helped confuse the enemy in the southern sector of the line as did BrigGen Koenig's diversionary moves against Qaret el Himeimat and Naqb Rala with his Free French Brigade.

When details began to filter into Montgomery's HQ early in the morning, he was rather pleased with the preliminary results. The attacks had gone reasonably well, although X Corps did not have as many tanks forward through the minefields as hoped. Enemy resistance had been fierce as had been expected, but progress had been made all along the line. If the bridgehead could be strengthened as planned, crumbling attacks could begin to grind down Axis infantry and provoke a showdown with the Panzer divisions. The outcome of the battle would then depend on who could best endure the battle of attrition that would follow.

Enemy casualties and kit lie scattered around a fortified position that had been overrun during Operation *Lightfoot*. These positions were difficult to see and to locate in the featureless desert, often remaining undetected by the advancing infantry until machine-gun fire ripped their ranks. (IWM E18657)

EL ALAMEIN: THE DOG FIGHT

awn on 24 October brought with it a fair degree of optimism regarding the results of the previous night, but daylight also introduced new problems for Montgomery's forces. During the morning all formations were trying to get their vehicles into the bridgehead that had been carved through the enemy minefields. Smoke, dust, shell fire and mines all helped to create a fog of battle that introduced an element of chaos into the proceedings. Six divisions from two corps were all attempting to clear gaps for their own use in an area that had no fixed boundaries or recognizable features, whilst all the while being harassed by an enemy who had not yet been fully evicted. It is not surprising then that traffic jams and frayed tempers began to influence decisions.

LtGen Montgomery intended to continue with the plan he had laid out before the battle. Work was to resume carving out the corridors on XXX Corps front. The 51st Division was to push on to its primary objective and help clear 1st Armoured Division's gaps. New Zealand Division was to get onto the Miteirya Ridge then exploit southwards. MajGen Gatehouse's 10th Armoured Division was ordered to advance with strong artillery support over the ridge to protect the New Zealanders' flank. Montgomery told LtGen Lumsden that he was prepared to accept casualties amongst his corps, but he had to get the tanks forward. On the extreme right flank the Australian Division would begin its crumbling operations northwards starting that night, the South Africans would do likewise on the other flank. In the far south, Horrocks was told that if 7th Armoured Division could not get through the second minefield, then 44th Division would have to force a gap with a night attack. Maximum air effort in support of ground forces that day was requested from AVM. Coningham and his aircraft rose to the occasion by flying over 1,000 sorties.

On the enemy side there was something approaching dismay. The attack had achieved complete surprise and for almost an hour after the assault had begun there was little response from the Axis artillery. The effects of British artillery, and the jamming of German radio frequencies, had disrupted Axis communications and resulted in most news of the attacks having to be relayed by messengers to senior commanders. It took time before an overall appreciation of the offensive could be built up at Panzerarmee HQ. The simultaneous attacks on the line from the sea to the Qattara Depression meant that its commander, Gen d.Kav Stumme, was unable to determine which thrust was the main one. He had surmised that the main British effort would be delivered just south of the centre, but no reports could confirm that this had in fact happened. Desperate to assess matters, Stumme set out for the front to see for himself. It was a mistake, for as he neared the sector of the line opposite

LtGen Montgomery with two of his armoured commanders. From left to right: Brig 'Pip' Roberts (22nd Armoured Brigade), Montgomery and MajGen Gatehouse (10th Armoured Division). (IWM E16484)

the Australians his staff car was shelled and he died of a heart attack. The loss of Stumme at this most critical time in the battle was a huge blow to the enemy.

For a while no one knew what had happened to Stumme, or where he was. By midday the awful realization that Panzerarmee Afrika was leaderless became apparent and command passed temporarily to Gen d.Pz von Thoma. He had no better idea of the true situation than had Stumme and decided to contain the British attacks locally rather than commit any of the armoured formations. In Berlin the crisis was also viewed with alarm at OKW. At around 1500hrs a message was sent to Rommel. He was summoned from his convalescence and ordered to return to Africa and take over the battle. He arrived late the following day.

Crew of a Crusader tank cook breakfast beside their tank in the early October morning sunshine. (IWM R16266)

Progress made by Eighth Army on 24 October was disappointing. Few tanks made it completely through the minefields in either of the armour's corridors. Only minor gains were made by 51st Division. The Highlanders put in an attack to clear a passage for MajGen Briggs' 1st Armoured Division in the afternoon, but although some tanks of 2nd Armoured Brigade got beyond the German obstacles, they remained well short of their objective, Kidney Ridge. Montgomery continued to urge his armoured commanders to get their divisions through the minefields and out into the open where they could manoeuvre, but little effort was made to comply with the order. LtGen Freyberg was incensed with MajGen Gatehouse's unwillingness to exploit the success of his infantry. The commander of 10th Armoured Division said that his tanks would be shot to pieces if they ventured over the ridge and he seemed preoccupied with getting his division into position to repel an enemy attack rather than to initiate one of his own. Further urging and pleading by Leese not to let the opportunity slip by, also failed to get the armoured divisions moving.

After a meeting with his commanders, Lumsden signalled Montgomery that his corps would attack that night. Montgomery signalled back that they must attack that afternoon. To comply with the army commander's wishes, Gatehouse's 8th Armoured Brigade sent a reconnaissance attack across the Miteirya Ridge at 1600hrs that afternoon only to find a new minefield covered by anti-tank guns. The half-hearted advance stopped three hours later when Lumsden signalled to his chief that the attack would resume later that night.

That night's operations by 10th Armoured Division had massive artillery support from the guns of the division and those of 51st and 2nd New Zealand Divisions. After a period of counter-battery fire and a heavy barrage, Gatehouse's two armoured brigades, the 8th and 24th, intended to advance over the top of the ridge supported by 133rd Lorried Infantry Brigade. When the attack got underway it immediately got caught up in the minefield along the crest of the Miteirya Ridge. Enemy shellfire hampered attempts to clear gaps and then the Luftwaffe put in an air attack on the waiting armour. The raid caused some disorganization as the armour dispersed for safety. When the attack tried to resume the artillery barrage had gone too far forward for the tanks to catch up with

British infantry on a daylight patrol near enemy lines. The flat open terrain of the desert made this a particularly hazardous task. (IWM E14582)

it and Brig Custance, commander 24th Brigade, advised the divisional commander that it was inadvisable to go on with the advance. Gatehouse agreed, fearful that daylight would find the division in some disarray, with tanks still on the forward slope or caught in the minefield. Freyberg was appalled with the decision; he needed armoured protection if his division was to exploit to the south and relayed the news of the delays to his corps commander.

When Leese reported this news to Eighth Army's HQ, the sleeping Montgomery was roused from his bed and became most annoyed at news of the setback. The army commander then met with his two corps commanders at his Tactical HQ at 0330hrs and told them both that 10th Armoured would break out that night as ordered. Monty also told Lumsden that he would have no hesitation in removing commanders if his orders were not carried out. This blunt speaking seemed to have some effect, for during the night news began to filter back that 24th Brigade had broken through into the open and was in contact with 2nd Armoured Brigade on its right. Ninth Armoured Brigade had also got through the minefield and was ready to support the New Zealanders in their crumbling operations the next day. LtGen Montgomery went back to bed thinking that his armour was at last out in the open ready to challenge the Panzer divisions and attack them.

The next morning it was soon realized that none of this had in fact happened and there was no armour whatsoever on the forward slopes of the Miteirya Ridge. The 1st Armoured Division also did not have 2nd Armoured Brigade on Kidney Ridge. To make matters worse, Horrocks had called off the attack by 7th Armoured Division in the south, citing problems in getting through the minefields.

In view of these failures, LtGen Freyberg reported that his division could not now start the crumbling attacks as planned. He had completely lost faith in the British armour and doubted whether Gatehouse would ever get his division to break out beyond the Miteirya Ridge. Freyberg even suggested that the New Zealand Division should put in an artillery supported attack with its own infantry to gain a position 4,000 metres beyond the ridge for Gatehouse's tanks. Monty refused, knowing that the attack would be costly for the infantry. He required these infantry for the crumbling operations that were to follow and was well aware of the high losses already suffered by the troops of three of the four divisions of XXX Corps that had forced their way through the minefields. Only the Australians were anything like near their full strength.

On the other side of the battlefield, Gen von Arnim had been puzzled by British actions since the battle began. The British had taken the advantage during the first night, but had declined to press this advantage the next morning or in the afternoon. This allowed the temporary commander of Panzerarmee to move more guns into the critical Miteirya area and to lay more mines. He predicted that the British would then attack that night, 24 October, with infantry. What in fact came at his forces in the dark was a huge artillery barrage and a half-hearted attack by armour. This convinced von Thoma that the thrust from the Miteirya Ridge was the main British effort and sent some of his tanks into the area to be ready for it.

Operation *Lightfoot* was not going according to plan for Montgomery. Although XXX Corps had almost reached most of its original objectives, the armoured divisions were just not performing. Casualties amongst the infantry, although not excessive, were still high and amounted to over 4,500. There were no reinforcements available for the New Zealand or South African Divisions, and

MajGen Briggs, Commander 1st Armoured Division (left) with LtGen Lumsden (right). Montgomery was not best pleased with the performance of his armoured commanders during the opening stages of the Alamein battle. (IWM E16464)

the Highland Division's casualties had reached 2,100. These losses had been suffered even though the enemy had not committed the whole Afrika Korps or 90th Light Division, although some tanks of 15th Panzer Division had been sent against the Miteirya Ridge area. Monty knew that the failure of a night attack by the New Zealand infantry or another refusal to implement his orders by the armoured commanders could result in stalemate, or worse, especially if the Panzer divisions were moved against him before his armoured divisions were in a position to receive them.

He decided to change his original plan. He needed to try to surprise the enemy and retain the initiative. In a bold move he now ordered the right-hand sector of the break-in to carry the main weight of the attack. He intended that the 1st Armoured Division would push forward to form a shield for the Australian Division who would then begin its crumbling operations northwards towards the sea. He hoped that this new line of attack would catch the enemy unawares and threaten to take the coast road. If the attack was successful, he could switch the whole axis of this advance to the north and the enemy would be compelled to move his Panzer divisions against it. In the meantime, 10th Armoured Division would be withdrawn, except for 24th Armoured Brigade which would join 1st Armoured Division. The remainder of XXX Corps would continue to hold the line along the Miteirya Ridge.

On 25 October, 1st Armoured Division attacked north-westwards but made little headway against enemy anti-tank defences. During the day it dealt with an attack by German and Italian armour, beating the enemy back with the loss of 34 of its own tanks. The Australians, meanwhile, continued with their preparations for the attack northwards. In the south, 50th Division attempted and failed to penetrate the enemy minefield on its front and 44th Division took over the ground that 7th Armoured Division had won. The disappointing results gained by XIII Corps did, however, have a wider significance in that its attacks had kept 21st Panzer and Ariete Divisions in the southern sector away from the main effort in the north.

On the night of 25/26 October the 51st Highland Division made ground towards its original objective line on 'Oxalic'. At the same time, a little further north, LtGen Morshead's 9th Australian Division attacked towards the strategically important ground at Point 29. This slight rise

gave good observation over the northern section of the battlefield with exceptionally good sight towards the coast. The assault was put in by 26th Australian Brigade supported by the Valentine tanks of 40th RTR and the guns of five field and two medium regiments of artillery. In the air 79 sorties were flown by Wellingtons and Albacores which dropped 115 tons of bombs on targets in the battle area. German fighters were kept at bay by night-flying Hurricanes. The Australian attack was a complete success and well before dawn the 26th Brigade had two battalions dug in on the feature ready to deal with any enemy counterattack.

GFM Rommel had arrived back at Panzerarmee's HQ the previous evening. He was shocked by what had happened since his departure and with the reports that were given to him regarding fuel and supplies. Little of what had been promised had been delivered. The lack of fuel worried him most, for the shortages restricted the mobility of his army just when he needed speed and manoeuvrability. When news arrived of the loss of Point 29, he ordered an immediate counterattack by elements of 15th Panzer and 164th Divisions, together with infantry and tanks from Italian XX Corps. He was concerned that this British success would be followed up by an armoured thrust north-west towards the coast road.

Rommel's counterattack was unsuccessful. His assembled forces were strafed and bombed the whole day and British and Australian Artillery broke up his formations as they approached Point 29, forcing the move to be abandoned. Later that day Rommel decided to move his reserve forward and brought 90th Light Division eastwards in front of Point 29. He also contemplated bringing 21st Panzer and Ariete Divisions north to reinforce the sector, but knew that if he did so he would not have enough fuel to move them back again.

The enemy reaction to the moves by the Australians had strengthened Montgomery's hand. Rommel was beginning to engage more and more of his tanks in countering each of the small gains made by Eighth Army. The fighting all along the front was grinding down Rommel's forces and eating away at his strength. Although Montgomery didn't fully realize it, the sheer size of the British attack was forcing Rommel to spend his force in penny packets. The field marshal's

THE DOG FIGHT

After Operation *Lightfoot* had broken into the German line, as far as Phase Line *Oxalic*, Gen Montgomery knew that he would have to engage the Axis armoured divisions in a 'dog fight' to draw off some of their strength prior to launching his breakout offensive, Operation *Supercharge*.

Note: Gridlines are shown at intervals of 2 miles

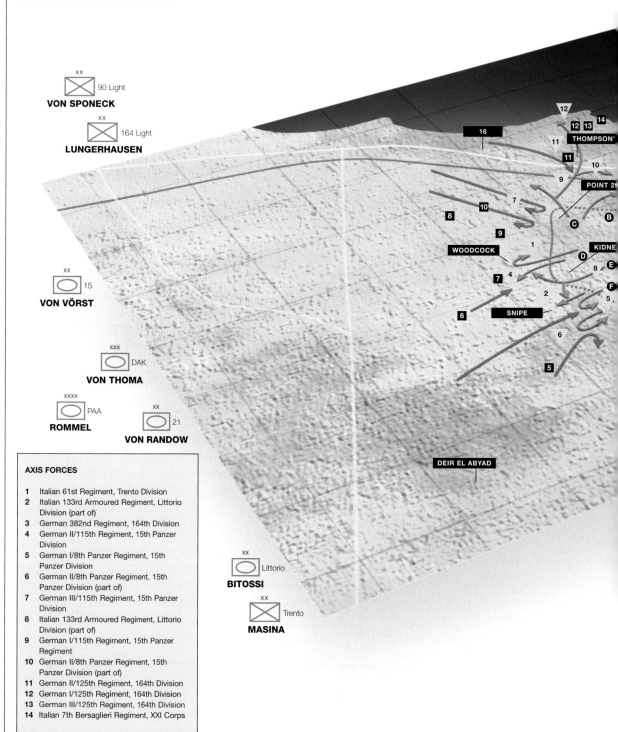

AXIS FORCES

1 Italian 61st Regiment, Trento Division
2 Italian 133rd Armoured Regiment, Littorio Division (part of)
3 German 382nd Regiment, 164th Division
4 German II/115th Regiment, 15th Panzer Division
5 German I/8th Panzer Regiment, 15th Panzer Division
6 German II/8th Panzer Regiment, 15th Panzer Division (part of)
7 German III/115th Regiment, 15th Panzer Division
8 Italian 133rd Armoured Regiment, Littorio Division (part of)
9 German I/115th Regiment, 15th Panzer Regiment
10 German II/8th Panzer Regiment, 15th Panzer Division (part of)
11 German II/125th Regiment, 164th Division
12 German I/125th Regiment, 164th Division
13 German III/125th Regiment, 164th Division
14 Italian 7th Bersaglieri Regiment, XXI Corps

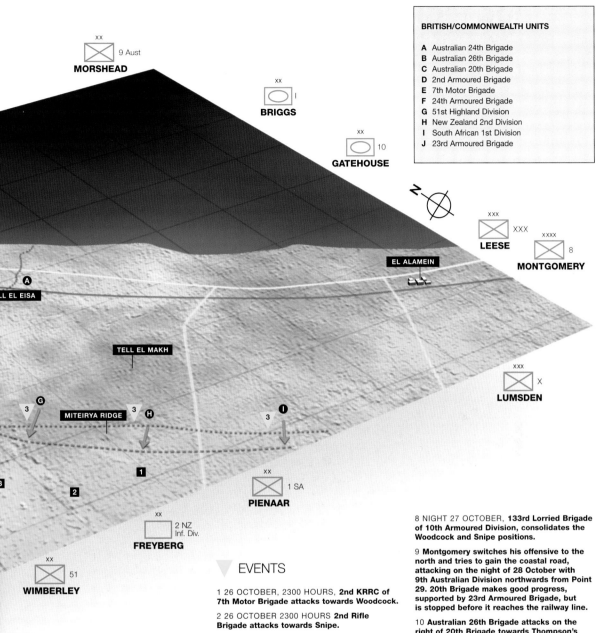

BRITISH/COMMONWEALTH UNITS

A Australian 24th Brigade
B Australian 26th Brigade
C Australian 20th Brigade
D 2nd Armoured Brigade
E 7th Motor Brigade
F 24th Armoured Brigade
G 51st Highland Division
H New Zealand 2nd Division
I South African 1st Division
J 23rd Armoured Brigade

MORSHEAD
9 Aust

BRIGGS

GATEHOUSE
10

LEESE

MONTGOMERY
8

EL ALAMEIN

LL EL EISA
A

TELL EL MAKH

LUMSDEN
X

MITEIRYA RIDGE
G   H   I
3   3   3

1

2

3

PIENAAR
1 SA

FREYBERG
2 NZ Inf. Div.

WIMBERLEY
51

▼ EVENTS

1 26 OCTOBER, 2300 HOURS, **2nd KRRC of 7th Motor Brigade attacks towards Woodcock.**

2 26 OCTOBER 2300 HOURS **2nd Rifle Brigade attacks towards Snipe.**

3 NIGHT 26/27 OCTOBER, **51st Division, New Zealand 2nd Division and South African 1st Division attack to extend the front southwards to conform with** *Lightfoot*'s **first objectives.**

4 27 OCTOBER, **2nd Armoured Brigade advances to pass round 2nd KRRC but is stopped by counter attack by 15th Panzer Division.**

5 27 OCTOBER, **24th Armoured Brigade attacks to the south of Snipe, but meets 8th Panzer Regiment.**

6 **21st Panzer Division and I/8th Panzer Regiment counter attack during the afternoon of 27 October, but fail to push back the British.**

7 **90th Light Division and 12th Bersaglieri Regiment attack Point 29 late afternoon of 27 October, but are repulsed by Australian 9th Division.**

8 NIGHT 27 OCTOBER, **133rd Lorried Brigade of 10th Armoured Division, consolidates the Woodcock and Snipe positions.**

9 **Montgomery switches his offensive to the north and tries to gain the coastal road, attacking on the night of 28 October with 9th Australian Division northwards from Point 29. 20th Brigade makes good progress, supported by 23rd Armoured Brigade, but is stopped before it reaches the railway line.**

10 **Australian 26th Brigade attacks on the right of 20th Brigade towards Thompson's Post. Heavy fighting follows in which German I/125th Regiment is virtually destroyed.**

11 **The two Australian attacks cause Rommel to switch some of his forces to the north on 29 October. German 90th Light Division is moved against the Australians to stop them gaining the coast road. Heavy fighting draws more German units into the area when elements of 21st Panzer Division join in the struggle.**

12 **A fresh attack by Australian 26th Brigade on night of 30 October clashes again with 90th Light Division, but manages to cross the railway line and coastal road to reach the sea. Rommel is certain that this attack will be followed by Eighth Army's main breakout battle in this sector, but Montgomery has by then decided to launch his Operation** *Supercharge* **further south near Woodcock and Snipe.**

strength was diminishing to a point where it was in danger of becoming critical. Fifteenth Panzer Division for instance was down to just 40 tanks.

Montgomery now decided that the Australians should renew their attack northwards again on the night of the 28th/29th. Before that, 1st Armoured Division would put in another attack against the area around Kidney Ridge with 7th Motor and 2nd Armoured Brigades, while 51st, New Zealand and South African Divisions cleared any of the enemy still holding out in their sectors and advanced to the original Oxalic line wherever they were short of it. Monty also decided to create a reserve ready to launch against the enemy at a time suitable for exploitation. XXX Corps was told to withdraw the New Zealand Division and 9th Armoured Brigade on 27 and 28 October to join 10th Armoured Division in this reserve and to hold its sector of the line by redistributing other formations within the corps. The 7th Armoured Division was also given warning of a move north to join the reserve.

While these moves were being organized, 1st Armoured Division began an advance from the northern corridor to draw onto itself some of the enemy armour and to help the Australians on its right. On the night of 26 October, 7th Motor Brigade made an attack against two centres of resistance either side of Kidney Ridge – 'Woodstock' in the north and 'Snipe' in the south – both located approximately 1.5 kilometres from the ridge itself. Woodstock became the objective of 2nd Kings Royal Rifle Corps; Snipe was the goal of 2nd Rifle Brigade. These night attacks were required to seize these locations before dawn to allow 2nd Armoured Brigade to pass around to the north and 24th Armoured Brigade to advance to the south.

The attack got underway as planned at 2300hrs on 26 October behind a barrage fired by all the guns of both X and XXX Corps. Both battalions of 7th Motor Brigade made a successful advance and established themselves on or near their objectives, although they found that the featureless terrain made it difficult to pinpoint their locations exactly. At around 0600hrs the 2nd and 24th Armoured Brigades began their advance. Their progress was slow in the face of increasing enemy resistance, but by midday both were close to the battalions of 7th Motor Brigade. The moves had attracted opposition from the Littorio Division and from elements of both of the German Panzer Divisions. During the day each side pounded the other continuously as the British tanks

attempted to gain a breakthrough. Rommel, in turn, recognized the growing danger of the British moves and was determined to push back the British away from his main defence line. He ordered an immediate attack against the Kidney Ridge area.

In the afternoon the situation facing 1st Armoured Division deteriorated rapidly as all three brigades suddenly found themselves dealing with a full-scale German armoured counterattack. Rommel's blow fell most heavily on the Snipe area and was met by the 6-pdr anti-tank guns of 2nd Rifle Brigade and 239th Anti-tank Battery RA. The defence put up by these units was brave and dogged. The battalion, in the words of the official history, 'stood its ground and did great execution, particularly amongst enemy tanks advancing against 24th Armoured Brigade'. More than once it seemed that the battalion would be wiped out, but it hung on defiantly. The heroic stand made by the 2nd Rifle Brigade defeated the enemy counterattack completely; the enemy could not endure the losses taken by his tanks and withdrew. The 2nd Rifle Brigade's commander, LtCol V. B. Turner, fully deserved the Victoria Cross awarded to him for the action. Axis attacks against Point 29 by German 90th Light Division also failed that day.

That night 133rd Lorried Brigade came forward to help hold on to the gains and deal with further small counterattacks against the positions. The next day the pressure on the enemy continued when Montgomery shifted his weight northwards and launched 9th Australian Division towards the coastal road. This new push opened on the night of 28 October with 20th Australian Brigade making a set-piece attack to enlarge the ground already taken around Point 29. A simultaneous assault by 26th Australian Brigade on the right striking northwards towards the railway line and the coastal road hoped to widen this penetration. Good progress was initially made in these attacks, but increasing enemy resistance stopped them both before they could reach their objectives. None the less, the attacks were deemed to be a success for they caused great destruction to the units of German 164th and 90th Divisions pitted

OPERATION SUPERCHARGE: THE BREAK OUT

Launched in the early hours of 2 November, Operation *Supercharge* was designed to penetrate Rommel's main line south of the salient formed by 9th Australian Division. Montgomery intended to use the reinforced New Zealand Division to punch a hole through the Axis positions, hold open the breach with 9th Armoured Brigade and allow X Corps to pass through.

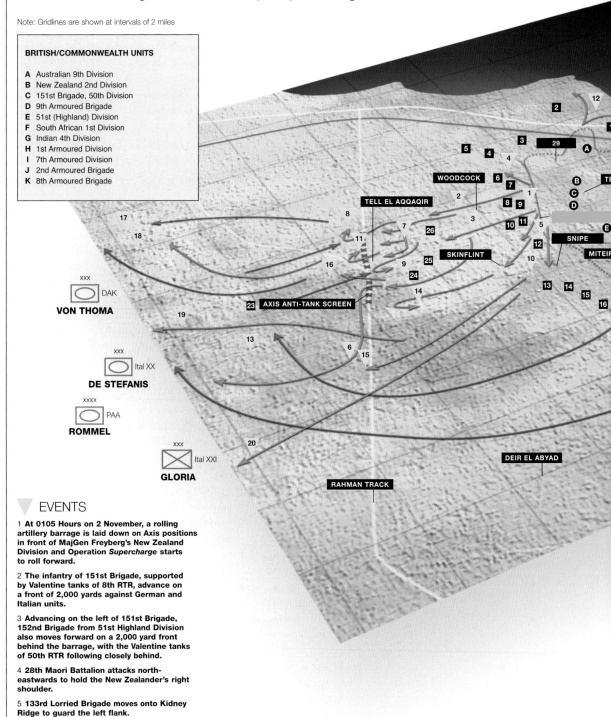

Note: Gridlines are shown at intervals of 2 miles

BRITISH/COMMONWEALTH UNITS

A Australian 9th Division
B New Zealand 2nd Division
C 151st Brigade, 50th Division
D 9th Armoured Brigade
E 51st (Highland) Division
F South African 1st Division
G Indian 4th Division
H 1st Armoured Division
I 7th Armoured Division
J 2nd Armoured Brigade
K 8th Armoured Brigade

WOODCOCK
TELL EL AQQAQIR
SKINFLINT
SNIPE
MITEIR
AXIS ANTI-TANK SCREEN

xxx
DAK
VON THOMA

xxx
Ital XX
DE STEFANIS

xxxx
PAA
ROMMEL

xxx
Ital XXI
GLORIA

DEIR EL ABYAD
RAHMAN TRACK

▼ EVENTS

1 **At 0105 Hours on 2 November, a rolling artillery barrage is laid down on Axis positions in front of MajGen Freyberg's New Zealand Division and Operation *Supercharge* starts to roll forward.**

2 **The infantry of 151st Brigade, supported by Valentine tanks of 8th RTR, advance on a front of 2,000 yards against German and Italian units.**

3 **Advancing on the left of 151st Brigade, 152nd Brigade from 51st Highland Division also moves forward on a 2,000 yard front behind the barrage, with the Valentine tanks of 50th RTR following closely behind.**

4 **28th Maori Battalion attacks north-eastwards to hold the New Zealander's right shoulder.**

5 **133rd Lorried Brigade moves onto Kidney Ridge to guard the left flank.**

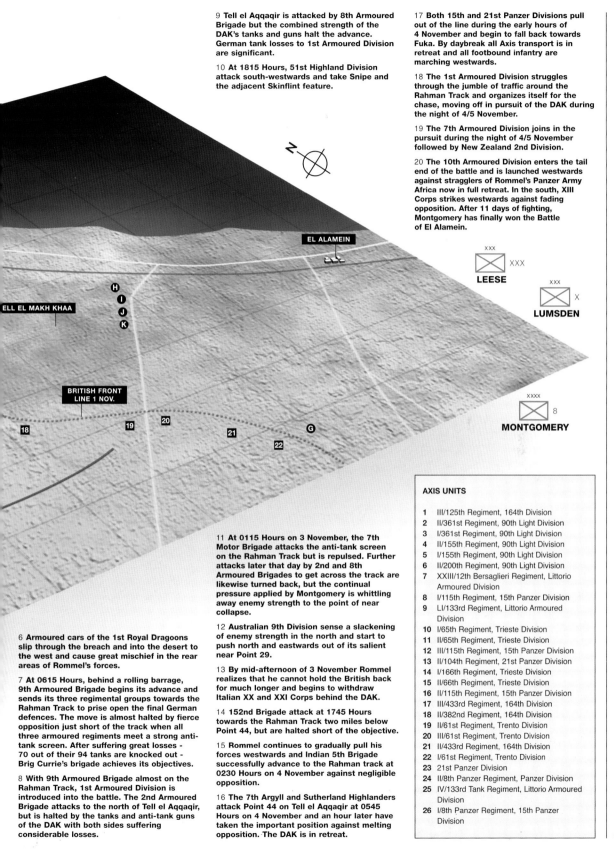

9 Tell el Aqqaqir is attacked by 8th Armoured Brigade but the combined strength of the DAK's tanks and guns halt the advance. German tank losses to 1st Armoured Division are significant.

10 At 1815 Hours, 51st Highland Division attack south-westwards and take Snipe and the adjacent Skinflint feature.

17 Both 15th and 21st Panzer Divisions pull out of the line during the early hours of 4 November and begin to fall back towards Fuka. By daybreak all Axis transport is in retreat and all footbound infantry are marching westwards.

18 The 1st Armoured Division struggles through the jumble of traffic around the Rahman Track and organizes itself for the chase, moving off in pursuit of the DAK during the night of 4/5 November.

19 The 7th Armoured Division joins in the pursuit during the night of 4/5 November followed by New Zealand 2nd Division.

20 The 10th Armoured Division enters the tail end of the battle and is launched westwards against stragglers of Rommel's Panzer Army Africa now in full retreat. In the south, XIII Corps strikes westwards against fading opposition. After 11 days of fighting, Montgomery has finally won the Battle of El Alamein.

EL ALAMEIN

LEESE

LUMSDEN

ELL EL MAKH KHAA

BRITISH FRONT LINE 1 NOV.

MONTGOMERY

11 At 0115 Hours on 3 November, the 7th Motor Brigade attacks the anti-tank screen on the Rahman Track but is repulsed. Further attacks later that day by 2nd and 8th Armoured Brigades to get across the track are likewise turned back, but the continual pressure applied by Montgomery is whittling away enemy strength to the point of near collapse.

12 Australian 9th Division sense a slackening of enemy strength in the north and start to push north and eastwards out of its salient near Point 29.

13 By mid-afternoon of 3 November Rommel realizes that he cannot hold the British back for much longer and begins to withdraw Italian XX and XXI Corps behind the DAK.

14 152nd Brigade attack at 1745 Hours towards the Rahman Track two miles below Point 44, but are halted short of the objective.

15 Rommel continues to gradually pull his forces westwards and Indian 5th Brigade successfully advance to the Rahman track at 0230 Hours on 4 November against negligible opposition.

16 The 7th Argyll and Sutherland Highlanders attack Point 44 on Tell el Aqqaqir at 0545 Hours on 4 November and an hour later have taken the important position against melting opposition. The DAK is in retreat.

6 Armoured cars of the 1st Royal Dragoons slip through the breach and into the desert to the west and cause great mischief in the rear areas of Rommel's forces.

7 At 0615 Hours, behind a rolling barrage, 9th Armoured Brigade begins its advance and sends its three regimental groups towards the Rahman Track to prise open the final German defences. The move is almost halted by fierce opposition just short of the track when all three armoured regiments meet a strong anti-tank screen. After suffering great losses - 70 out of their 94 tanks are knocked out - Brig Currie's brigade achieves its objectives.

8 With 9th Armoured Brigade almost on the Rahman Track, 1st Armoured Division is introduced into the battle. The 2nd Armoured Brigade attacks to the north of Tell el Aqqaqir, but is halted by the tanks and anti-tank guns of the DAK with both sides suffering considerable losses.

AXIS UNITS

1	III/125th Regiment, 164th Division
2	II/361st Regiment, 90th Light Division
3	I/361st Regiment, 90th Light Division
4	II/155th Regiment, 90th Light Division
5	I/155th Regiment, 90th Light Division
6	II/200th Regiment, 90th Light Division
7	XXIII/12th Bersaglieri Regiment, Littorio Armoured Division
8	I/115th Regiment, 15th Panzer Division
9	LI/133rd Regiment, Littorio Armoured Division
10	I/65th Regiment, Trieste Division
11	II/65th Regiment, Trieste Division
12	III/115th Regiment, 15th Panzer Division
13	II/104th Regiment, 21st Panzer Division
14	I/166th Regiment, Trieste Division
15	II/66th Regiment, Trieste Division
16	II/115th Regiment, 15th Panzer Division
17	III/433rd Regiment, 164th Division
18	II/382nd Regiment, 164th Division
19	II/61st Regiment, Trento Division
20	III/61st Regiment, Trento Division
21	II/433rd Regiment, 164th Division
22	I/61st Regiment, Trento Division
23	21st Panzer Division
24	II/8th Panzer Regiment, Panzer Division
25	IV/133rd Tank Regiment, Littorio Armoured Division
26	I/8th Panzer Regiment, 15th Panzer Division

against them. Armour from 15th Panzer Division was also attracted northwards to help stem the attack.

The two Australian attacks caused Rommel to switch more and more of his forces to the north. On 29 October elements of 21st Panzer Division came up from the south and joined in the struggle against the Australians. The fighting in this northern sector led Montgomery to contemplate making his breakthrough here. His divisions were engaged in a dog fight in which his superior strength and resources must prevail. He now decided that he would move the New Zealand Division into the area to maintain the momentum of the infantry attacks, prior to launching his armoured reserve in a breakout battle along the coast road.

A fresh attack by Australian 26th Brigade on the night of 30 October clashed again with 90th Light Division and did great execution. The advance continued across the railway line and coastal road to reach the sea. It then attempted to turn eastwards to capture a defended locality called Thompson's Post, encircling the First Battalion of German 125th Regiment. Although the attacks did not achieve all that was planned, they did form a salient across the road and railway line through which the trapped enemy forces found it difficult to withdraw. These moves made Rommel certain that this attack would be followed by Eighth Army's main breakout attempt through this salient towards Sidi Abd el Rahman and for a brief moment he considered making a general withdrawal to a new line at Fuka. He decided to withdraw 21st Panzer Division to an area north of Point 44 at Tel el Aqqaqir to form a mobile reserve. Rommel knew that he would need this reserve to counter any possible break-through in the north. More bad news arrived at his HQ that day when he heard that the tanker *Luisiano* had been sunk and little more fuel would reach his army in the near future.

Rommel had read Montgomery's thoughts correctly when he predicted that the British might try to break through in the north, but by then Eighth Army's commander had changed his mind again. The main effort would now go through south of this sector. Montgomery had formulated a new plan for his great breakout battle, one which, in his words, 'would hit Rommel for six'.

EL ALAMEIN: BREAKOUT AND PURSUIT

LtGen Montgomery's new plan for the breakout was called *Supercharge* and was similar in concept to *Lightfoot*: XXX Corps' infantry would attack in strength at night followed closely by the armour. Simultaneously, in the south, Horrocks' depleted XIII Corps would lead the enemy into thinking that an attack was going in there. The location and direction of *Supercharge* would be out of a 4,000-metre front just to the south of the Australian-held ground around Point 29. As before there would be tremendous support from both artillery and the aircraft of the Desert Air Force. There was one added advantage in that there would be no deep minefields to contend with during the initial attack. Mines would be present, but only in scattered patches. This time, Montgomery insisted, armour would be passed through the infantry without any loss of momentum.

The New Zealand Division would carry out the initial infantry attack, strengthened by the addition of several other formations. It would make the assault with 151st Brigade from 50th Division and 152nd Brigade from 51st Division under command, both with a battalion of tanks in support. Following closely behind would be 9th Armoured Brigade, also under LtGen Freyberg's command. This brigade would carry the attack from the infantry's objective for another two kilometres behind a rolling barrage to smash through and capture the enemy defences around the Rahman track. The momentum would then be taken up by 1st Armoured Division who would take on the Panzer divisions backed by its

Gen Montgomery in a classic pose standing in the turret of his Grant tank. With his black beret on his head and binoculars in hand this was the image flashed around the world during his moment of victory. (IWM E18980)

**THE ACTION FOUGHT BY THE 3RD KING'S OWN HUSSARS
NEAR THE RAHMAN TRACK ON 2 NOVEMBER DURING
OPERATION** *SUPERCHARGE* (pages 84–85)

Montgomery's final battle to break through Rommel's
positions at Alamein, Operation *Supercharge*, began late on
1 November with an attack by the reinforced New Zealand
Division. At 0615 Hours the next day, behind a rolling
barrage, 9th Armoured Brigade took up the advance with
orders to break through the enemy anti-tank and field-gun
positions to 'hold the door open' for the 1st Armoured
Division of X Corps. Montgomery told the commander, Brig
Currie, that he was prepared to take 100 per cent casualties in order for the brigade to reach the Rahman track.
When the CO of The 3rd The King's Own Hussars, Lt Col Sir
Peter Farquhar, protested that 'this was just suicide,'
Montgomery remained adamant. The advance by the 3rd
King's Own Hussars is recognized as one of the greatest
armoured regimental actions of the war. The Hussars faced
fierce enemy opposition and shellfire during the whole of
the operation. On the move up to the start line alone, it lost
most of its carriers and soft-skinned vehicles to shell fire.
By the time it had arrived on the infantry objective ready
to begin its own attack, ten of its tanks had been
destroyed. The Hussars battled their way forward and
eventually reached the Rahman Track at first light.
Unfortunately, at this critical time, the tanks became
silhouetted against the dawn sky and drew heavy anti-tank
fire. The Hussars pressed on relentlessly through this

barrage, driving straight at the German gun positions,
crushing the enemy weapons beneath their tracks. At very
close quarters, the tanks were fought to a standstill, having
to eliminate each anti-tank gun in turn whilst the Germans
returned this fire at point blank range. Soon the battlefield
was a mass of burning armour and broken guns, with the
Hussars left with just seven serviceable tanks out of the
35 that had set off earlier that morning. But the regiment
had gained its objective and broken through the Axis anti-
tank line along the Rahman Track just as they had been
ordered to do, allowing X Corps a route through the
German defences. It was the turning point of Operation
Supercharge. The battlescene shows the 3rd King's Own
Hussars at the height of the action when their tanks had
closed right up to the enemy anti-tank gun positions. By
this time in the Alamein battle the Hussars had received
some of the newly arrived Sherman tanks (1) and were
using them to good effect. The mainstay of the regiment
were the sturdy Grants (2) and their 75mm and 37mm
weapons were particularly useful in this close combat. Also
present in the action were the near-obsolete Crusaders (3),
but their speed counted for little in this type of battle and
most quickly became casualties. The enemy PAK 38 5cm
anti-tank gun (4) was one of the enemy's most useful and
reliable weapons and did sterling service for the German
Army throughout the war. Close by is a burning Panzer II
(5), a tank totally outclassed on the battlefield, but still
useful as a reconnaissance and close-support weapon
for the field guns. (Howard Gerrard)

anti-tank guns. Either side of this main attack, other divisions would simultaneously whittle away at the Axis defences, probing for an opening through which to exploit.

At 0105hrs on 2 November, Operation *Supercharge* got underway behind an artillery barrage laid down on Axis positions. Prior to this, starting at 2115hrs the previous evening, AVM Coningham's aircraft had begun seven hours of attacks on enemy locations along their line. The Royal Navy also played a part in the operation by simulating landings along the coast, dropping rafts and flares from torpedo boats and filling the air with tracer fire and noise.

The infantry of 151st Brigade, supported by Valentine tanks of 8th RTR, began its advance on a front of 2,000 metres against German and Italian defences. Advancing on their right, 152nd Brigade also moved out behind a rolling barrage, with the Valentine tanks of 50th RTR following closely behind. On the right of these attacks, New Zealand 28th Maori Battalion attacked north-eastwards to hold the northern shoulder of the assault. To the south, the 133rd Lorried Brigade carried out the same defensive task around Kidney Ridge.

The ground attack started well, with both brigades advancing through 4,000 metres of enemy defences to reach their objectives without excessive loss. Taking immediate advantage of the advance, two armoured car regiments tried to slip through the breach out into open country. One, 1st Royal Dragoons, was especially successful and two of its squadrons got out into the desert to the west and caused great mischief in the rear areas of Rommel's forces.

At 0615hrs, behind a rolling barrage, 9th Armoured Brigade split into three groups and took over the advance towards the Rahman Track, aiming to prise open the final German defences. Montgomery had told 9th Brigade's commander, Brig Currie, that he was prepared to take 100 per cent casualties, but the brigade had to get onto the Rahman track. The brigade rose to this challenge and, although almost halted by fierce opposition and a strong anti-tank screen in front of the track, reached

EIGHTH ARMY DRIVE

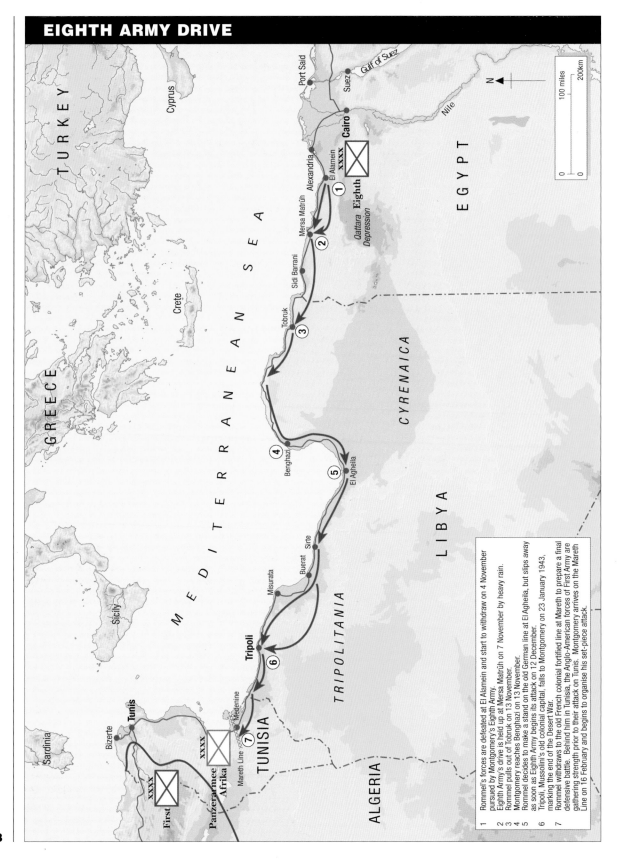

1 Rommel's forces are defeated at El Alamein and start to withdraw on 4 November pursued by Montgomery's Eighth Army.
2 Eighth Army's drive is held up at Mersa Matrûh on 7 November by heavy rain.
3 Rommel pulls out of Tobruk on 13 November.
4 Montgomery reaches Benghazi on 13 November.
5 Rommel decides to make a stand on the old German line at El Agheila, but slips away as soon as Eighth Army begins its attack on 12 December.
6 Tripoli, Mussolini's old colonial capital, falls to Montgomery on 23 January 1943, marking the end of the Desert War.
7 Rommel withdraws to the old French colonial fortified line at Mareth to prepare a final defensive battle. Behind him in Tunisia, the Anglo-American forces of First Army are gathering strength prior to their attack on Tunis. Montgomery arrives on the Mareth Line on 16 February and begins to organise his set-piece attack.

88

German and Italian prisoners of war are escorted into captivity. When Rommel's forces collapsed at the end of the battle, most of those troops who got away had their own transport. Those infantry who had no access to vehicles, and this included the bulk of the Italian infantry divisions, had to try to make their escape on foot. Thousands of them were captured. (IWM E18485)

its objectives. Losses were substantial – 70 out of their 94 tanks were knocked out – but the dash of Brig Currie's brigade cracked open the enemy line in what has since been recognized as one of the greatest cavalry achievements of the war.

With 9th Armoured Brigade on the Rahman Track, 1st Armoured Division came forward to be introduced into the battle. The 2nd Armoured Brigade attacked to the north of Tel El Aqqaqir, but was halted by the tanks and anti-tank guns of the Afrika Korps with both sides suffering considerable losses. The defences on Point 44 at Tel El Aqqaqir were then attacked by 8th Armoured Brigade which had been transferred to the division for the battle from 10th Armoured Division. The combined strength of the enemy tanks and guns proved to be enough to halt this advance as well, but the Panzer Korps suffered significant losses.

Elsewhere the Axis line was beginning to buckle. Later in the day at 1815 hrs, 51st Highland Division advanced south-westwards to take *Snipe* and the adjacent *Skinflint* feature. Fighting continued through the night. At 0115 hrs on 3rd November, the 7th Motor Brigade attacked the anti-tank screen on the Rahman Track, but was repulsed. Further attacks later that day by 2nd and 8th Armoured Brigades to get across the track were likewise turned back, but the continual pressure applied by Montgomery was whittling away enemy strength to the point of near collapse.

To the north, Australian 9th Division sensed a slackening of enemy resistance and started to push north and eastwards out of its salient near Point 29. By mid-afternoon of 3 November, Rommel realized that he could not hold the British back for much longer and took the heavy decision to begin to withdraw Italian XX and XXI Corps behind the Afrika Korps, but still the British attacks came at him. When Hitler learned of the withdrawals he was furious and ordered Rommel to stand firm. No retreat by any formation was permitted. Rommel reversed his order and prepared for his forces to meet their *Valhalla*. The pressure continued when the 152nd Brigade tried a new assault at 1715hrs towards the Rahman track, three kilometres below Point 44. Rommel's forces halted it just short of its objective.

Axis resistance to the British moves two days into the operation was still dogged, but Montgomery knew that the battle of attrition was swinging in his favour. The enemy was pulling back, but he still did not realize that Rommel's army was so close to the point of collapse. Indian 5th Brigade was now brought northwards to join in the battle and successfully advanced to the Rahman track at 0230hrs on 4 November against negligible opposition. A little later the 7th Argyll and Sutherland Highlanders attacked Point 44 on Tel El Aqqaqir at 0545hrs and an hour later took the strategically important position against melting opposition. Rommel knew that he was beaten. Urgings from Hitler had little effect on his army's resolve, his formations were gradually recoiling westwards; Panzerarmee Afrika was in retreat. Both 15th and 21st Panzer Divisions pulled out of the line during the early hours of 4 November and began to stream back towards Fuka. By daybreak all Axis transport was in full retreat and all footbound infantry that managed to disengage themselves from the fighting were marching westwards.

Montgomery decided that it was now time to unleash his mobile forces. The 1st Armoured Division struggled through the jumble of traffic around the Rahman track and organized itself for the chase, moving off in pursuit of the Afrika Korps on the night of 4/5 November. Then 7th Armoured Division joined in the pursuit during the night followed by New Zealand 2nd Division at first light. Eighth Army Commander then decided that MajGen Gatehouse's 10th Armoured Division could now enter the tail end of the battle and he launched it westwards against the stragglers of Rommel's army now in full flight. In the south XIII Corps was striking out into the desert against fading opposition. After eleven days of fighting, and the loss of 13,560 men killed, wounded and missing, Montgomery had won the Battle of El Alamein.

A great victory had been achieved at El Alamein, but the pursuit of Rommel's beaten army was not the great triumph for Eighth Army that it should have been. Disorganized, fragmented, demoralized and short of fuel, Panzerarmee Afrika was ripe for the *coup de grace* and the vastly superior Eighth Army should have delivered it. For many reasons, some complex and real, others fanciful and apologetic, Montgomery allowed Rommel's forces to slip away along the coast of North Africa. By 13 November Rommel was at Tobruk and a week later in Benghazi. The further west the Axis forces travelled the shorter their supply lines became. The withdrawal was not a rout, but it was a full retreat. There was no longer any hope that Panzerarmee Afrika would ever attain enough strength to go back on to the offensive. Its fate was finally sealed on 8 November when Anglo-American forces landed in Algeria and Morocco and then moved swiftly into Tunisia. Rommel now had an Allied army to his front and rear. The inevitable end of the Desert War came on 13 May 1943 when all those Axis forces that were still fighting on the continent of Africa surrendered to Gen Eisenhower's forces. GFM Erwin Rommel was not among them; the Desert Fox had slipped away to Italy to fight another day.

THE BATTLEFIELD TODAY

The open and featureless desert south of the small railway station of El Alamein has changed little in the sixty years since the battles of 1942; it still remains a most desolate region. The same cannot be said for the stretch of coastline from Alexandria to El Alamein. This has become an almost continuous strip of development. El Alamein itself has also changed and is now a small town of around 5,000 people with a port facility for shipping oil nearby. There are also several small hotels and a beach amenity in the neighbourhood. The tiny railway station beloved of war photographers in 1942 as the only place bearing the name of El Alamein has been replaced by a very modern structure a short distance away, although the old single-story building remains *in situ*.

El Alamein is quite accessible for tourists and is located just over 100 kilometres from Alexandria. To cater for visitors who come to see just where one of the most important battles of the Second World War took place, a museum has been built. Here the battle is explained in dioramas, photographic displays and contemporary exhibits. Those visitors more interested in hardware will find relics of the opposing forces also on show, with examples of the tanks and guns that fought in the battle on display around the outside of the building.

There are several difficulties to be encountered for those who wish to leave the roads and get out into the desert to reach the more remote areas of the battlefield. The area of desert to the south of the coastal road and railway line is vast and most inhospitable for the unwary. It is still devoid of people and settlements, empty save for the few locals who

One of the dangers that still mar the Alamein battlefield today. Wind and weather has uncovered this anti-tank mine, but many of the hundreds of thousands that were laid in 1942 still remain buried and make the whole area very dangerous to the unwary. (Robin Neillands)

criss-cross the area along the ancient tracks that traverse the sands. It is also a very difficult area to get to. This is not the place for tourists in hire cars to go for a drive, for soft ground, deep gullies and shifting sands can trap the uninitiated. There is also considerable danger from the hundreds of thousands of mines that were laid by both sides during the conflict, many of which still remain, untouched and unlocated.

The most suitable way to experience the detail of the battlefield is with one of the reputable battlefield tour companies who organize visits to site. They will make the arrangements, devise a programme, lay on guest speakers, organize guides and arrange suitable transport. All you then have to do is to enjoy the locations and relive the action. These companies usually have great experience in organizing these trips; they have all done it before and will be prepared for any eventuality. Dates, itineraries and costs can be found on their various web pages on the Internet.

As with all battlefields, the most poignant sites of all are the war cemeteries and mausoleums. There are three in the area, one for British and Commonwealth dead, one for the German fallen and one for Italian victims of the fighting. All are, as you would expect, calm peaceful oases in the parched desert. The British cemetery, administered by the Commonwealth War Graves Commission, looks out from Alamein towards the Miteirya Ridge from a position close by the museum. There are over 8,000 burials located here, together with a roll of names of those who have no known grave. Between the stark headstones there is none of the soft grass that is found in European cemeteries, only wind-blown sand. At the top of the cemetery is an impressive shrine made up of a series of cloisters stretching for almost 90 metres.

The Axis dead are commemorated on two separate sites. The 33-metre high Italian monument was built in 1959 and is situated in an area of 1,500 square metres of ground leased out to the Italian government for 99 years. The names of 4,634 soldiers are inscribed on the mausoleum's walls. The German memorial is shaped like a medieval Teutonic castle and stands on a ridge at Tel el Eisa near the sea. In its inner courtyard a tall obelisk supported by four falcons is ringed by memorial plates and mosaic panels listing the names of 4,200 German dead.

BIBLIOGRAPHY

Bierman, John & Smith, Colin, *Alamein: War Without Hate*, Viking, London (2002)

Blaxland, Gregory, *The Plain Cook and the Great Showman*, Kimber, London (1977)

Braddock, D. W., *The Campaigns in Egypt and Libya*, Gale & Polden, Aldershot (1964)

Carver, Michael, *Dilemmas of the Desert War*, Batsford, London (1986)

Carver, Michael, *El Alamein*, Batsford, London (1962)

Delaney, John, *Fighting The Desert Fox*, Arms & Armour, London (1998)

Forty, George, *The Armies of Rommel*, Arms & Armour, London (1997)

Gilbert, Adrian (ed), *The IWM Book of the Desert War*, Sidgwick & Jackson, London (1992)

Hamilton, Nigel, *Monty: The Making of a General 1887–1942*, Hamish Hamilton, London (1981)

Horrocks, LtGen Sir Brian, *A Full Life*, Collins, London (1960)

Irving, David, *The Trail of the Fox*, Weidenfeld & Nicolson, London (1977)

Joslen, LtCol H. F., *Orders of Battle: Second World War 1939–1945*, HMSO London (1960)

Kippenberger, MajGen Sir Howard, *Infantry Brigadier*, Oxford University Press, Oxford (1949)

Liddell Hart, B.H. (ed), *The Rommel Papers*, Collins, London (1953)

Lucas, James, *Panzer Army Africa*, Macdonald & Janes, London (1977)

Messenger, Charles, *The Unknown Alamein*, Ian Allen, Shepperton (1982)

Montgomery, Field Marshal The Viscount, *El Alamein to the River Sangro*, Hutchinson, London (1948)

Pimlott, Dr John, *Rommel In his Own Words*, Greenhill, London (1994)

Playfair, MajGen I.S.O., *The Mediterranean and Middle East Volume III,* HMSO, London (1960)

Playfair, MajGen I.S.O., *The Mediterranean and Middle East Volume IV,* HMSO, London (1966)

Quarrie, Bruce, *Afrika Korps*, Patrick Stephens, Cambridge (1975)

Quarrie, Bruce, *Panzers in the Desert*, Patrick Stephens, Cambridge (1978)

Ryder, Rowland, *Oliver Leese*, Hamish Hamilton, London (1987)

Stewart, Adrian, *The Early Battles of Eighth Army*, Leo Cooper, Barnsley (2002)

INDEX

References to illustrations are shown
in **bold**.

Alam Haifa, Battle of 11, 31, 45–47,
    50–51, 53–55, **56–58**, 59
    aftermath **54**
Alam Haifa Ridge 12, 30, 47, 53
Alamein, First (battle of) 10–11, **12**,
    12, 15, 20, 24, 30, 32, 34-35, **36–38**,
    39–44, 45 *see also* El Alamein, Battle
    of
Alamein Box 34, 35, 41, 42
Alexander, Gen the Hon Sir Harold
    7, 7, 11, 12, 15–16, 26, 45, 60, 61
Alexandria 34
Arena, Gen Francesco **18**
Arnim, Gen von 73–74
artillery barrage **68**
artillery crew, German **23**
Auchinleck, Gen Sir Claude 8,
    10–11, 12, **15**, 15, 20, 22, 29–30, **35**,
    45, 47
    First Alamein 35, 39, 40, 41, 42,
        43, 44
Axis forces 23–26, 32 *see also* German
    forces; Italian forces
    casualties **70**
    Order of Battle 28

Bab el Qattara 32, 34, 35, 41, 65
Bastico, Marshal Ettore 17, 29
Bayerlein, Oberst Fritz **18**, **51**, 51
Bismarck, GenMaj Georg von **19**, **51**,
    51, 66
Briggs, MajGen R. 26, **74**
British forces 7, 20–23 *see also* Desert
    Air Force
    Argyll and Sutherland Highlanders,
        7th 90
    armoured brigades
        2nd 72, 78, 89
        4th 40
        8th 50, 54, 72, 89
        9th 14, 60, 68, 69, 73, 83, **84–86**,
            87, 89
        22nd 47
        23rd 45, 47, 50, 53, **58**, 68
        24th 72, 73, 74, 78
    Armoured Division, 1st 13, 26, 45,
        73, 74, 78, 79, 83, 87, 89, 90
        First Alamein 35, **36–38**, 39, 40, 42
        El Alamein, Battle of: the attack
            60, 66, 67, 70
    Armoured Division, 7th (Desert

Rats) 20–21, **21**, 26, 43, 60, 66,
    70, 71, 73, 78, 90
    Alam Haifa, Battle of 45, 50, 51,
        55
Armoured Division, 8th 26, 60, 66
Armoured Division, 10th **8**, 26, 60,
    66, 67, 70, 71, 72, 73, 74, 90
armoured divisions 22
Australian 9th Division **12**, 12, 13,
    26, 45, 55, 71, 74, 79, 89
    First Alamein 41–42, 44
    El Alamein, Battle of: the attack
        66, 67, 68
Australian Brigade, 20th 79
Australian Brigade, 26th 75, 79, 82
brigades
    131st 47
    132nd 47, 55, 59
    133rd 47, 79, 87
    151st 55, 83, 87
    152nd 83, 87
Corps, X 13, 14, 16, 21, 26, 60, 62,
    66, 69–70, 78
Corps, XIII 13, **16**, 21, 26, 45, 46,
    74, 83, 90
    First Alamein 34, 35, **36–38**, 39,
        40, 41, 42
    El Alamein, Battle of: the attack
        61, 66, 67, 70
Corps, XXX 12, **15**, 21, 26, 73, 74,
    78, 83
    First Alamein 35, 42
    Alam Haifa, Battle of 50, 54
    El Alamein, Battle of: the attack
        61, 66, 67, 68–69
Division, 44th 26, 47, 66, 71, 74
Division, 50th 26, 66, 74
Eighth Army 8, 10, 11, 12, 14,
    20–21, 22, 23, 26, 30
    First Alamein 42, 44
    Alam Haifa, Battle of 45, 46, 47
    El Alamein, Battle of 60, 61, 72,
        90
(Highland) Division, 51st 26, 66,
    67, 68–69, 71, 72, 74, 89
Indian 4th Division 26, 66, 67, 69
Indian 5th Brigade 54–55, 90
Indian 5th Division 35, 42, 43, 44, 45
Indian 18th Brigade 35
infantry **73**
infantry divisions 22
King's Own Hussars, 3rd **84–86**
King's Royal Rifle Corps, 2nd 78
Light Armoured Brigade, 4th 50

Maori Battalion, 28th 87
Motor Brigade, 7th 40, 50, 78, 89
New Zealand 2nd Division 12, 14,
    26, 71, 72, 73, 82, 83, 87, 90
    First Alamein 35, **36–38**, 39, 40,
        42, 43, 44
    Alam Haifa, Battle of 45, 47,
        54–55
    El Alamein, Battle of: the attack
        60, 66, 67, 69
New Zealand 4th Brigade 42-43
New Zealand 6th Division 55, 59
officers **10**, **12**
Order of Battle 26
Rifle Brigade, 2nd 78, 79
Royal Artillery 61, 67–68
    239th Anti-Tank Battery 79
Royal Dragoons, 1st 87
Royal Engineers **69**
Royal Tank Regiment, 40th 75
sergeant **62**
South African 1st Division 26, **27**,
    35, 41, 42, 45, 66, 67, 69
South African 2nd Brigade 54
South African 2nd Division 12
tank crew, Crusader **72**
Brooke, Gen Sir Alan 45–46
Burrows, Brig 43

Cairo 10, 31, 32, 34, 62
Cavallero, Marshal Ugo 17, **18**, 29,
    50, 55, 66
cemeteries, war **90**, 93
chronology 12–14
Churchill, Winston **7**, 15, 30, 44,
    45–46, 61
Clifton, Brig 59
commanders, Axis 17–19
commanders, British 15–17
Coningham, AVM 62, 71, 87
Cunningham, Gen Alan 8
Currie, Brig 69, **86**, 87
Custance, Brig 73
Cyrenaica 7, 8, 61

de Stefanis, Gen Giuseppe **19**, 19, 28
Deir el Shein 35, 39, 40, 44, 45
Desert Air Force 23, 34, 35, 43, 46,
    53–54, 62, 68, 83
Desert War 7–8, 15, 91

Eden, Sir Anthony **17**
Egypt 7, 8, 10, 29, 45
El Agheila 7, 8, 14

El Alamein 92
  railway station **32**, 32, 92, **93**
El Alamein, Battle of 11, 14 *see also*
  Alamein, First
  origins 7–8, 10-11
  the attack 60–63, 65–70
  the dog fight 71–75, 78–79, 82
  breakout and pursuit 83, 87, 89–91
  battlefield today **66**, **92**, 92–93
El Alamein line 10, 12, 29, 32, 34, 35,
  39
equipment: 'jerrycans' **27**

Farquhar, LtCol Sir Peter **86**
Fellers, Col Bonner 31
'foxholes' **30**
Frattini, Gen Enrico 28
French, Free, 1st Brigade 22, 66, 67,
  70
French, Free, 2nd Brigade 22
Freyberg, LtGen Sir Bernard, VC
  16–17, **17**, 26, 59, 69, 72, 73, 83

Gairdner, MajGen C.H. 26
Gatehouse, MajGen A.H. **8**, 26, **71**,
  72, 73
Gazala, Battle of 17, 20, 32
German forces
  Afrika Korps 8, 12, 13, 23, 28, 29,
    34, 45 *see also* German forces:
      Panzer Divisions, 15th and 21st
    Alam Haifa, Battle of 47, 50, 51, 53
    armoured divisions 25
    First Alamein **36–38**, 39, 40
    officers **29**
  artillery crew **23**
  Brigade, 152nd 89
  Light Division, 90th 10, 12, 23, 25,
    28, 63, 75, 79, 82
    First Alamein 34, 35, 41
    Alam Haifa, Battle of 45, 47, 53,
      54
  Light 'Afrika' Division, 164th 23,
    25, 28, 42, 45, 55, 63, 75, 79, 82
  officers **29**
  Order of Battle 28
  Panzer Division, 15th 8, 23, 34, 42,
    63, 74, 75, 76, 82, 90
    Alam Haifa, Battle of 53, 54,
      56–58
  Panzer Division, 21st 8, 12, 23, 34,
    39, 41, 44, 63, 82, 90
    Alam Haifa, Battle of 53, 54, **58**
  Panzer Regiment, 5th **19**, 44
    Panzerwerkstattkompanie **13**
  Panzer Regiment, 8th **27**, 42, 44
  Panzerarmee Afrika 7, 10, 14, 23, 25,
    29, 40, 43, 46, 59, 60, 62, 65, 90, 91
  Panzergrenadiers **6**, 34, **45**, **46**
  Parachute Brigade, 288th 45, 65
  Regiment, 125th 82
  Regiment, 382nd 42
  soldier **30**
Gloria, Gen Alessandro 28

Gott, LtGen 'Strafer' **16**, 35, 46
Graziani, Gen Marshal 7
Greece 8
Greek Brigade, 1st 21-22

'Hammerforce' 66
Harding, MajGen A.F. 26, 61
Hitler, Adolf 7, 10, 17, 89, 90
Horrocks, LtGen Brian **16**, 26, 46,
  71, 73
Hughes, MajGen I.T.P. 26

infantry, British **73**
Infantry Tactics 17
Italian forces 7-8, 24–25
  air force (Regia Aeronautica) 23
  Corps, X 28, **36–38**, 39, 45, 65
  Corps, XX 24, 28, 34, 39, 45, 53,
    63, 75, 89
  Corps, XXI 28, 34, 45, 63, 89
  divisions
    Ariete 24, **36–38**, 39, **41**, 47, 54,
      63
    armoured 24, 25
    Bologna 63, 65
    Brescia **36–38**, 39, 42, 44, 45, 65
    Folgore Parachute 45, 65
    infantry 24
    Littorio 12, 24, **41**, 47, 54, 63, 78
    Pavia 42, 65
    Sabratha 41
    Trento 63
    Trieste 24, **41**, 54, 63
  generals 19
  gun crew **25**
  infantry **14**
  Order of Battle 28
  signalmen **63**
  tank commander **36–38**
  troops **43**

Kesselring, Generfeldmarschall
  Albert 17, **18**, 29, 50, 55
Kidney Ridge 72, 73, 78, 79, 87
Koening, BrigGen 70

Leese, LtGen Sir Oliver **15**, **16**, 16,
  26, 61, 69, 73
Libya 7, 8
Luftwaffe 23
  troops **34**
Luisiano 82
Lumsden, LtGen Herbert **16**, 16, 26,
  60, 71, 72, 73, **74**

Malta 61
Mellenthin, Oberstleutnant **18**
Mersa Matruh 10, 12, 34
mine-clearance teams, Royal
  Engineer **69**
minefields 51, 65
mines, anti-tank **30**, **43**, **45**, **92**
Miteirya Ridge 63, 67, 69, 70, 71, 72,
  73, 74, **90**

Montgomery, LtGen Sir Bernard **7**,
  13, 14, **16**, 16, 26, **71**, **83**
  arrival 11, 12, 15, 16, 21, 30–31,
    45–46, 47
  Alam Haifa, Battle of 50, 53, 54,
    55, 59, 60
  El Alamein, Battle of 60, 62, 70,
    71, 72, 73, 74, 78, 79, 82, 83, 90-91
  corps de chasse 60
Morshead, LtGen Sir Leslie **15**, 17,
  26

Nehring, GenLt Walther **18**, 18, 35,
  51, 65
Nichols, MajGen J.S. 26

O'Connor, LtGen 7
officers, British **10**, **12**
officers, German **29**
Operation *Crusader* 8
Operation *Lightfoot* 8, 12, 66, **68**, **70**,
  74
Operation *Supercharge* 14, 83, **84–86**,
  87, 89–91
'Oxalic' position 66, 68, 69, 74, 78

Panzergrenadiers **6**, 34, **45**, **46**
Pienaar, MajGen D.H. **15**, 17, 26
plans, opposing 29-31
Point 29: 74, 75, 79, 83, 89
Point 44: 82, 89, 90
prisoners of war, German and Italian
  89

Qattara Depression 32, **62**

radio intercepts and signals 31, 31,
  41, 42, 47
Rahman Track 83, **84–86**, 87, 89, 90
Ramsden, LtGen W.H. 41, 61
Randow, GenMaj Heinz von 66
Renton, MajGen 61
Ritchie, LtGen Neil 8, 10, 12, **15**
Roberts, Brig 'Pip' **71**
Robertson, Brig 59
Rommel, GFM Erwin 12, 13, 14, **17**,
  17–18, **18**, 20, **24**, 25, **51**, 91
  origins of battle 7, 8, 10, 11
  advance towards Nile 29–30
  orders received 32, 34
  and Battle of Alam Haifa 31, 46,
    47, 50, 51, 55
  First Alamein 35, 39, 40, 41, 42,
    43, 44
  ill health 63, 66
  El Alamein, Battle of 62, 63, 65,
    72, 75, 78, 79, 82, 89, 90
Royal Navy, Mediterranean Fleet 34
Ruweisat Ridge 12, 34, 35, **36–38**, 39,
  40–41, 42, 43, 44, 45, 46, 47, 67

sand storm **12**
sergeant, British **62**
signalmen, Italian **63**